A Way with Words
Book 1

TEACHER'S BOOK

A Way with Words
Vocabulary development activities for learners of English

Book 1

TEACHER'S BOOK

Stuart Redman and Robert Ellis

Advisory editor: Michael McCarthy

CAMBRIDGE
UNIVERSITY PRESS

Published by the Press Syndicate of the University of Cambridge
The Pitt Building, Trumpington Street, Cambridge CB2 1RP
40 West 20th Street, New York, NY 10011-4211, USA
10 Stamford Road, Oakleigh, Melbourne 3166, Australia

© Cambridge University Press 1990

First published 1990
Third printing 1994

Printed in Great Britain
by Athenæum Press Ltd, Newcastle upon Tyne

ISBN 0 521 35918 X   Teacher's Book
ISBN 0 521 35917 1   Student's Book
ISBN 0 521 35026 3   Cassette

GO

Contents

Thanks

We are grateful to a number of people who have helped us with this book. In particular our thanks to:

    our editor at CUP, Jeanne McCarten, and our advisory editor, Mike McCarthy, who have supported us throughout this project with knowledge, guidance, and great enthusiasm – their contribution has been immense;

Ruth Gairns for her ideas and comments on the material, and also for the personal support that she and Eun Bahng have given us during the development of this book over the past two years;

the teachers at The London School of English and The Bell Language Institute, London, and the teachers in the schools and colleges in various parts of the world who have all piloted this material and provided us with such important feedback;

Michael Swan for his valuable comments on the pilot manuscript;

and finally to Judith Aguda, our desk editor, and the rest of the staff at CUP who have helped to make this book possible.

Introduction

A Way with Words Book 1 is the first in a series of three books designed to answer the student's perennial question: 'How can I learn more vocabulary?' In doing this it provides a new approach to vocabulary acquisition – an approach which is different from previous vocabulary books in a whole variety of ways.

How is it different?

○ It recognises that vocabulary does not just mean single words: compounds, phrases and even, on occasion, whole sentences can be *items* of vocabulary. And it recognises that items of vocabulary form related sets and do not occur at random within conversations and texts. (Units 3.3, 6.4 and 14.1 provide examples of this.)

○ It consciously teaches students about ways of learning vocabulary so that they become keenly aware of every opportunity for vocabulary expansion which presents itself. (The exercises in Unit 1 introduce the students to key aspects of learning, and many of the *Self-study activities* reinforce this emphasis.)

○ It encourages creative involvement in the process of learning vocabulary in the classroom. The teacher's role is to see that students take full advantage of dictionaries, context, fellow students, mother-tongue, knowledge of the world and so on. Almost all the exercises in the book encourage this kind of self reliance.

○ It encourages the same sort of involvement in studying alone: every unit provides a separate section of *Self-study activities* specifically designed for self-access. The teacher is also encouraged to photocopy the student-friendly Key in the Teacher's Book so that many other exercises become accessible to students studying alone or correcting their own work in class.

○ It contains a huge variety of exercise types, many of which are based on recent insights into how vocabulary is acquired. In this way it caters for a whole range of learning styles and keeps students constantly motivated.

○ It contains word building tables and grammatical explanations in a separate appendix to alert students to the rules governing vocabulary formation and use.

○ There is an accompanying cassette containing recordings for the listening exercises which present new items of vocabulary. It also provides vital help with the pronunciation of difficult or key items.

○ Finally, *A Way with Words* is different because it brings vocabulary teaching into the mainstream of English Language Teaching. It applies both tried and tested criteria and new techniques to an aspect of ELT which has for too long been considered something of a mystery.

Who is it for?

Book 1 was written for lower-intermediate students – students who have perhaps studied a beginners' coursebook and have now gained the confidence to speak, write, read and listen to a lot more English; they only lack the words. At a slightly higher level students may also welcome the opportunity to learn 'basic' words that have somehow slipped through the net, and many of the exercises are designed to be 'open-ended' so that these students need not feel that the activities are 'too easy' for them.

A Way with Words Book 1 is designed to be flexible. It can be used: to supplement a general English course; for a vocabulary option; for self-access; or to add variety to a reading or listening class. We even know some teachers who think they could use it as a coursebook – and some students who agree!

How is it organised?

There are eighteen units in three groups of six. All the units deal with topics which might typically be included in the main coursebooks at this level. The units are not graded in any way, so you or your students can pick out the appropriate topic at any stage. And if you want to follow up a particular topic (or topics) and recycle some of the new items which have been introduced, there are three *Revision and expansion* units – the last unit in each group of six: Units 6, 12 and 18.

What vocabulary does it teach?

Each unit actively introduces about 60 items (about 1,000 in the book as a whole), though full exploitation of the open-ended exercises will substantially increase this number.

The selection of vocabulary is based on the following:

1 Published wordlists such as *The Cambridge English Lexicon* by Roland Hindmarsh (1980, CUP) and the *General Service List of English Words* by Michael West (1953, Longman).
2 English language coursebooks at this level such as the *Cambridge English Course Book 2* by Michael Swan and Catherine Walter (1985, CUP).
3 Our own experience (and that of other teachers) of the needs, interests and problems of learners of English at this level.

Of course, the final selection is a subjective one and certain types of exercise tend to attract less useful items to the high frequency items which are being introduced. Nevertheless, the final selection represents a vocabulary corpus which is relevant and appropriate for learners at this level.

What does a unit consist of?

Most units provide five exercises plus a sixth which deals with pronunciation problems. Each exercise is split into sections so that classes/students can spend as little as perhaps twenty minutes or as much as three hours on a unit if everything is fully exploited. An exercise will typically begin with a section designed as a first introduction to the items to be learned. But a brief introduction is rarely enough to find out how an item is used, where it is used, what its limitations are, how it behaves in certain situations, what other words are likely to co-occur and so on. And, even more importantly, a brief introduction alone guarantees that the student will forget the item just as quickly as he or she 'learned' it! It is with this in mind that (in parts b, c and d of each exercise) the students are engaged in staged practice activities which may involve one or more of the four skills.

This description of a 'typical' exercise is somewhat misleading. The exercises provide an enormous variety of ways to meet and get to know new vocabulary. There are exercises based on problem-solving, grouping words, situations, pictures, sentence-building, ordering, grammar, pronunciation, reading, listening, dialogues, discussion, morphology, opposites, spelling, dictionaries, errors, and so on.

How is practice related to theory?

The choice of exercise types is not random. Good teaching is based on sound theory – and here this must mean both lexical theory and learning theory. Here are some examples of how theory becomes practice in *A Way with Words*:

○ The native-speaker's choice of vocabulary is often used to help structure spoken discourse. Synonyms, hyponyms, antonyms and meronyms all frequently take this role in real speech. See, for example, Units 7.4, 8.3 and 14.4, where this feature of language is exploited through the students' imitation of formulaic patterns. The repeated 'pattern' and contextualisation also act as memory aids.

○ *Lexical cohesion* in structuring written text can be a complex matter, but the simple substitution of a word by a synonym avoids repetition and binds different parts of the text to each other. In Unit 8.4 this aspect of discourse is highlighted and serves as a vehicle to introduce certain synonyms through their use in an authentic context.

○ The ability to *paraphrase* is a vital skill for any language learner; realistically, he or she will never know all the words they need. Useful tools are provided in, for example, Units 2.6 and 12.8.

○ In the real world students first seek a *translation* (with or without the help of a dictionary) when they meet a new item of vocabulary. In *A Way with Words* this fact is not ignored. Instead, the pitfalls are indicated and practical help is given in efficient use of the dictionary, for example in Units 10.4 and 11.4.

○ A knowledge and awareness of lexical features such as *compounding* and *affixation* can help learners to expand their vocabulary quickly and easily. This can be achieved not only by using previous knowledge of the language in the formation of new words, but also by applying some imaginative guesswork. The generative potential of these features is recognised and encouraged in Units 5.1, 8.1 and 12.12.

○ *Countability, transitivity* and the behaviour of *multiword verbs* are often dealt with as grammatical features of the language but there is a danger that students will not see these as aspects of the 'lexical grammar' of the words they learn. Special attention is paid to these areas not only in the appendix to *A Way with Words*, but also in, for example, Units 2.2, 8.2 and 6.10 where their importance is highlighted.

○ It is widely recognised that practice activities which involve the *learner's own ideas* and knowledge of the real world are highly motivating and thus are powerful aids to memory. Units 4.3, 5.5, 7.3 and 10.4 are just a few of many activities throughout this book which take full advantage of this fact.

○ The fact that certain words frequently *collocate* can be interpreted in a very narrow sense (where the words occur next to each other) or loosely (where the words occur within the same text). The whole range of interpretations is fully exploited in *A Way with Words* (see, for example, Units 6.7, 9.2, 10.2 and 11.1) because both theory and practice strongly suggest that items which are learned in relation to each other are more easily remembered than words in isolation.

There is not sufficient room here for further discussion of these matters so we refer the interested teacher to the Further reading and especially to *Working with Words* (Gairns and Redman, CUP, 1986).

Further reading

Gairns, Ruth and Redman, Stuart, *Working with Words*, Cambridge University Press, 1986.

Morgan, John and Rinvolucri, Mario, *Vocabulary*, Oxford University Press, 1986.

Carter, Ronald and McCarthy, Michael, *Vocabulary and Language Teaching*, Longman, 1988.

Wallace, Michael, *Teaching Vocabulary*, Heinemann Educational Books, 1982.

Carter, Ronald, *Vocabulary: Applied Linguistics Perspectives*, Allen & Unwin, 1987.

French Allen, Virginia, *Techniques in Learning Vocabulary*, Oxford University Press, 1983.

1 Learning: Teacher's notes

—— 1 Some natural ways of remembering words ——

a When the students have completed the first activity, you may need to explain one or two items from the box. The main purpose of the experiment, however, is to highlight the importance of organisation in vocabulary learning, i.e. if the students impose some kind of meaningful order upon the barrage of new words which they may encounter in an arbitrary way, they are more likely to be able to retrieve them from their memory. This means adopting some kind of system for recording new items (in a notebook, on a computer, or on a cassette), and initially it may seem like very hard work to some students. The point will therefore require regular reinforcement, both verbally and through vocabulary activities which involve organising recent input into meaningful units.

b The second part is really a fun activity, although it can sometimes lead to interesting discussion on the associations that these words trigger in the students' minds.

—— 2 Asking questions about the words you learn ——

Students need certain information about new vocabulary items, and it can be frustrating for them and time-consuming for you if they are unable to formulate the appropriate questions to obtain this information. This activity provides initial practice, but it should be repeated at regular intervals throughout the course, just for five minutes at a time. And as you repeat the activity for new items of vocabulary you can also introduce new questions to ask. With a group of verbs, for example:

i) Is it regular or irregular?
ii) Is it transitive or intransitive?
iii) Does it have more than one meaning?

You can also occasionally concentrate on just one aspect at a time such as spelling or pronunciation. Ask students to think of words for their partners to spell or to write lists of words for them to pronounce.

—— 3 Words to use when you are learning words ——

The final part of this activity can offer some interesting insights into the language learning beliefs and habits of your students, as well as providing free practice for the vocabulary presented in the earlier parts of the exercise.

——— 4 Keeping a record of the words you learn ———

a When students record new vocabulary, they tend to write one-word translation equivalents. For many items this will be an accurate and efficient way of recording meaning. For some items, however, translation equivalents will be inaccurate and misleading. For this reason students should be encouraged to consider different ways of recording meaning, and be made aware of the fact that sometimes a translation and/or a definition is needed, plus examples. For example, the word *afraid* has different meanings and different syntactic features governing its use. For this reason example sentences are important:

i) I'm afraid I can't come. (**not** I'm afraid *but* I can't come.)
ii) I'm afraid *of* the dark.

b When the students have completed the activity, discuss the answers with the class as a whole. This may take some time, but it will be worthwhile if it helps to establish clear principles about recording meaning. With a monolingual group it can be very interesting to discuss the validity of different translation equivalents.

——— 5 Finding your way round the book ———

This is an opportunity for the students to become familiar with the contents of the book so they will be able to locate the vocabulary relevant to their own needs and make use of the information contained at the back of the book.

Exercise **a** invites students to connect different sentences with different topics. The main aim is not that they should arrive at a *correct* answer, but that they are able to give logical reasons for their choice. This activity also provides an opportunity for very natural practice of the structures *must be*, *could be* and *can't be*.

The focus of exercise **b** is on the *Grammar* notes and *Word building tables* contained at the back of the book. It may take some time for students to read through these sections and check their answers, so this would make an ideal homework activity which you could then check in the next lesson. Unlike most of the units which present vocabulary within clearly defined topic fields, the vocabulary in this unit is very mixed (the emphasis being on vocabulary learning skills). Ask your students to deploy some of these skills and reorganise the lexical input from the unit. Can they organise some of the vocabulary into meaningful topic groups? Are there any items which present a similar problem in either comprehension or use? Are there items with specific pronunciation problems? Can they remember certain items together because they contain a common sound? And so on. You could distribute photocopies of the list of words and expressions at the end of the notes for this unit, to make this task a little easier.

6 Check your pronunciation

In your classroom teaching you will obviously need to practise the pronunciation of difficult items as they arise in the text. This exercise provides further reinforcement by grouping together a selection of the most difficult words and phrases from the unit. It can be incorporated into your teaching in a number of ways:

i) Use it in full for consolidation and revision.

ii) Give the final part of the exercise for homework and encourage your students, if possible, to record their sentences on to a cassette. If this practice is repeated throughout the course, your students will be developing their own cassette library; this offers another system for helping them to record and remember new vocabulary. It can be great fun.

iii) When the students have completed the exercise, ask them to find six more words or phrases from the unit which have pronunciation difficulties. The class can then discuss why these words are difficult to pronounce.

iv) Begin the unit with this exercise. As the words will be new, the students can only guess at the correct spelling. However, this is still a valid activity because students need to develop their ability to predict sound and spelling combinations. You may not wish your students to look through the unit in detail at this point, so write the correct spelling on the board (after the students have tried to write the words themselves), and give the students a very brief explanation of new items.

SELF-STUDY ACTIVITIES

1 This is another opportunity for your students to learn by imposing meaningful organisation on new input, and it is the type of activity that can be repeated for both learning and revision purposes.

2 The suggestions here are examples of the type of activity students can pursue in their own time to help them with vocabulary learning. We would suggest that you conduct a class feedback to find out if they have taken up either of the suggestions, and that you repeat the activity almost immediately. A little bit of encouragement and perseverance can do much to help establish a new habit, although in the long term these strategies will only prove valuable if they are adopted willingly and positively by the students.

You could also invite your students to make their own suggestions for simple learning/remembering strategies. No single idea will work for everyone, so the more suggestions you have the better.

1 Learning: Key words and expressions

Nouns

rabbit	flight
experiment	employee
brain	promotion
nightmare	pork
accident	sewing
examination	oven
pyjamas	spare time
politics	landing card
Christmas	launderette
recipe	plug
gap	rug
paper clip	performance
performance	department
five pound	store
note	ankle
dream	
owner	

Verbs

associate
fill in
  (a form)
rewrite
look (a word)
  up (in a
  dictionary)
cover
underline
overtake
equal
break down
break into
wrap (it) up
bite
book (a flight)
afford
leave
guess
rewrite

Verbs and nouns

explain/explanation
choose/choice
revise/revision
concentrate/
  concentration
expand/expansion
translate/translation
pronounce/
  pronunciation
improve/improvement
understand/
  understanding

Other words and expressions

What does (this word) mean?
How do you spell (this word)?
How do you pronounce (this word)?
How do you do?
What's the matter?
on the tip of my tongue

too (= as well)
therefore
hang on
I'm sorry I'm late

on holiday
on purpose
between
impolite

1 **Learning:** Key

—— 3 ——

a *explain:* give the meaning of a word or idea
concentrate: keep your attention on one thing
choose: select from different possibilities
expand: become or get larger
translate: change from one language into another
improve: get better
revise: study something again
understand: know the meaning of something

b *explain* → explanation   *translate* → translation
concentrate → concentration   *improve* → improvement
choose → choice   *revise* → revision
expand → expansion   *understand* → understanding

c 1 translation   4 revise   7 chose
  2 understand   5 expand   8 improve
  3 explanation   6 concentrate

—— 4 ——

b A translation would be suitable for: pork, overtake, plug.
  Example sentences would be suitable for: too, therefore, on purpose,
    equals, What's the matter?, leave.
  An explanation would be suitable for: launderette, rug, pork.
  A picture would be suitable for: overtake, plug, between.

»»»→

5

a 1 Work or Time
2 Money or Around the house
3 Entertainment or Time
4 Work or Transport
5 Sport and leisure or Clothes and shopping
6 Holidays and travel or Bureaucracy
7 Clothes and shopping or People and relationships
8 Food and drink or Around the house
9 Crime or Holidays and travel
10 Sport and leisure or Places

b The incorrect sentences should be rewritten like this:

1 It beg*a*n to rain.
4 He comes from Munich so he must be *German*.
6 I know this word because I looked *it up* in my dictionary.
7 I want to book my *flight*.
9 I can't afford a car but I want *one*.
10 It was terrible weather.

Sentences 2, 3, 5 and 8 are correct.

2 **Around the house:** Teacher's notes

—— 1 ————————————————————————————————

a Students can work on this exercise individually or in pairs before you produce a standardised version with the class. Vocabulary networks of this type are a simple and efficient way of recording vocabulary, and you could follow up this activity by asking students to create one of their own. The following example illustrates how certain household items could be revised through a network organised along different principles.

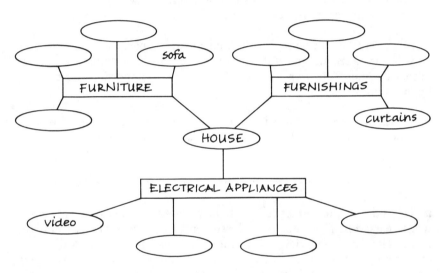

b This is a more abstract and personalised way of making connections between different items of vocabulary. Put the students in groups and encourage them to add more ideas of their own.

—— 2 ————————————————————————————————

a At this stage you may not wish to engage your students in a lengthy explanation of multiword verbs. If that is the case, just choose two familiar verbs, e.g. *put on / take off*, and demonstrate the position of the pronoun when used with these verbs, i.e. 'take *it* off' (and not 'take off *it*'). This knowledge is crucial if the students are to complete the following exercise correctly.

3

Begin by practising the pronunciation of difficult items – unfamiliarity with *stale* /steɪl/, *cupboard* /kʌbəd/, *wardrobe* /wɔ:drəʊb/ and *drawer* /drɔ:(ə)/ is almost certain to cause errors in pronunciation. Then put the students into pairs and allow them to use dictionaries to look up words they do not know. When they have exhausted the possibilities for different sentences, check the answers with the class.

4

a This is a preparation for the listening in **b** and it will be much easier for the students if they *write down* their ideas about the two types of accommodation shown in the picture.

b [▭] Play the tape once. Ask the students to compare their answers, and play the tape a second time if they have omitted any important information or they disagree. Afterwards you could highlight the important vocabulary on the board.

c This activity can be omitted if you are short of time, although it does provide important freer practice to consolidate the target vocabulary.

5

a Try and elicit the correct verb with the whole class, and explain any new words, e.g. *mess*. Then encourage the students to get up and move round the class. Tell them to interview at least three students and fill in the grid accordingly, either with names, or simply ticks as shown. With multilingual groups, in particular, this may lead on to some interesting class discussion; with a monolingual group the results may be too predictable to warrant much discussion.

6

a *Thing(s)* and *stuff* are extremely useful all-purpose words, particularly for lower level students with a limited vocabulary. This exercise provides initial practice but reinforcement will be necessary. For example, ask each student to bring to class a *thing* or some *stuff* which they cannot name in English. Practise in the following way, e.g.:

Student: What do you call this thing in English?
You: That's a plug.

SELF-STUDY ACTIVITIES

1 Students are often surprised at the number of words which can be generated from this simple activity. Inevitably they will sometimes produce incorrect compounds but this should not deter you; experimentation is an essential part of language learning, and your students will have a very real motivation (prompted by curiosity) to use their dictionaries in a productive way. They will also need to use dictionaries to find out how the compound is written – as one word, two words, or with a hyphen. There are no fixed rules here and even dictionaries vary.

2 Tell the students they must choose an object which they can explain in English. Initially some students are likely to forget to learn a word, but with perseverance they will remember, and once the practice is established it can become a regular activity and provide you with a very useful warm-up activity for the beginning of the lesson.

2 Around the house:
Key words and expressions

Nouns		Verbs	Adjectives
saucepan	coat hanger	daydream	broken
shower	lipstick	tidy (it) up	damp
sofa	plaster	turn (it) on	clean
towel	aftershave	turn (it) off	dirty
alarm clock	corkscrew	hang (it) up	empty
kettle	serviette	switch (it) on	stale (bread)
sheet	tablemat	switch (it) off	
sink	toothpick	turn (it) up	
washbasin	flour	turn (it) down	
coffee table	glue	put (it) out	
tumble dryer	bin	wake (him/her) up	
cupboard	freezer	melt	
dishwasher	chest of drawers		
wardrobe	privacy		
lift	noise		
block of flats	detached house		
lounge	stereo		
video	fridge		
computer	washing machine		

Other words and expressions

have an argument	do the cleaning	It's a thing you use for –ing.
waste time	do the ironing	It's the stuff you use for –ing.
feel relaxed	make a mess	a security risk
do the shopping	make a decision	I can look out onto the garden.
do the washing-up	make money	overlooking the city
do the cooking	make the bed	

2 Around the house: Key

a

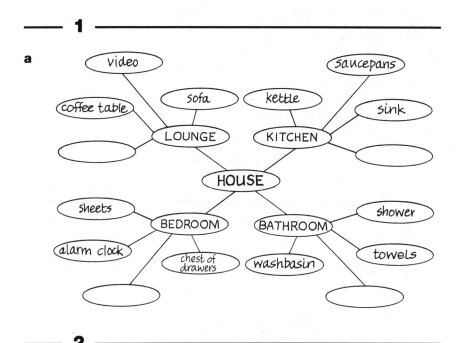

— 2 —

a
1 Hang it up.	6 OK, I'll tidy it up.
2 I'll wake him up.	7 OK, I'll turn it on.
3 OK, I'll turn it up.	8 That music is very loud.
4 Yes, I'll turn it off.	9 The light's off.
5 Yes, I'll put it out.	

b *washing machine:* turn it on/off, switch it on/off
stereo: turn it on/off, switch it on/off, turn it up/down
kettle: turn it on/off, switch it on/off
fire: turn it on/off, switch it on/off, turn it up/down, put it out
clothes: tidy them up, hang them up
computer: turn it on/off, switch it on/off
things: tidy them up, hang them up

—— 3

All these are possible answers:

The shirt was damp so I put it in the tumble dryer.
The shirt was clean so I put it in the drawer/wardrobe.
The plate was dirty so I put it in the dishwasher.
The plate was clean so I put it in the cupboard.
The plate was broken so I put it in the bin.
The ice cream was melting so I put it in the fridge.
The butter was melting so I put it in the fridge.
The bread was stale so I put it in the bin.
The bottle was broken so I put it in the bin.
The knife was broken so I put it in the bin.
The knife was clean so I put it in the drawer.
The knife was dirty so I put it in the dishwasher.

—— 4

b

Advantages	Disadvantages
1 a nice view quiet	no garden difficult to get to know people might get stuck in the lift
2 more privacy a garden	security risk

—— 5

We say:

do the shopping	*make* the bed(s)	*make* the most mess
do the washing-up	*do* the cleaning	*do* the ironing
do the cooking	*make* the most money	*make* most of the decisions

—— 6

a 1 the paint
   2 the sunglasses

SELF-STUDY ACTIVITIES

1 Here are some examples, but there are more:

living room	timetable	armchair
waiting room	dressing table	dining chair
classroom	dining table	wheelchair
bathroom	coffee table	deckchair

© Cambridge University Press 1990

3 Clothes and shopping:
Teacher's notes

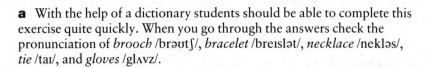

1

a With the help of a dictionary students should be able to complete this exercise quite quickly. When you go through the answers check the pronunciation of *brooch* /brəʊtʃ/, *bracelet* /breɪslət/, *necklace* /nekləs/, *tie* /taɪ/, and *gloves* /glʌvz/.

b A further extension to this is to ask your students to wear something special to the next class, e.g. earrings that were a present, something they bought on holiday, etc. In groups they can then talk about these items of clothing.

2

a Tell the students to use each item of vocabulary at least once. With a multilingual class it is advisable to bring something *suede* and *silk* into the class, otherwise these words will be very difficult to explain. If you work in a very hot climate or very cold climate, you may wish to change some of the vocabulary in order to make it more relevant to your students. In this case, write the items on the board.

b This activity could be omitted if you are short of time.

3

a Make sure your students understand what is expected of them in this activity. There is only one correct order for each conversation, but the sequence of the three conversations does permit two or three possibilities. If the students work in pairs, check the pronunciation of *blouse* /blaʊz/ before they start.

b The classroom now becomes a shop. Encourage the students to move about freely and use vocabulary from the previous exercises in this unit. This role-play often creates the need for *too + adjective*, e.g. *too tight/narrow/wide*, and so on. You could introduce this construction before you start if you feel you are not overloading your students with too much new input.

4

a Dictionaries will give the students a general understanding of these new words, but you may need to consolidate this understanding with further examples, e.g. types of *disease*; a situation to illustrate *protect*.

Make sure the students do not look at the text while they are discussing these questions.

b Elicit or explain the meaning of *originally* and *since then*, and highlight the tenses used with these items. Before the students write their own passages, you may wish to provide a further example, e.g. 'Originally I worked in a bank. Since then I've had a number of jobs, but now I enjoy being a teacher.'

c Explain the word *headline*. This may alert your students to the fact that one of the answers is contained in the headline.

5

a Impose a time limit, e.g. ten minutes, for this first activity.

b [cassette icon] Play the tape and ask the students to make a note of any differences between their answer and what they hear.

6

The words in the box are arranged in eight pairs of opposites, so students may be able to deduce unknown items from known items, e.g. if they understand *hard-working* then *lazy* should not be a problem. Tell the students to complete each sentence with a suitable adjective and then put them into small groups to discuss their answers.

SELF-STUDY ACTIVITIES

1 This is designed to encourage students to think in English outside the classroom. You could extend it by asking for other examples of information/instructions in their own language which they could translate into English, e.g. road signs and information, or instructions on medicine.
2 Check the answers in the next lesson. These are all common utterances in *shopping* situations and should be learned as fixed phrases.
3 Follow up this self-study activity with a brief class discussion. Apart from the lexical content this is a particularly useful exercise if your students have recently arrived in Britain or are planning to visit Britain.

3 Clothes and shopping:
Key words and expressions

Nouns		Adjectives	Verbs
earrings	shoulders	thick	wear
gloves	cotton	thin	try on
socks	leather	woollen	protect
tie	suede	(un)friendly	frighten
belt	silk	lazy	
scarf	suit	shy	
necklace	blouse	self-confident	
brooch	changing-room	(un)tidy	
cap	tribe	hard-working	
bracelet	disease	optimistic	
waist	folk music	pessimistic	
wrist	musical instrument	stupid	
neck	toys	(dis)organised	
chest	stationery	conservative	
needle and thread	envelope	intelligent	
underwear	skirt	adventurous	
shop assistant	tracksuit	fashionable	
customer	overcoat	attractive	
novel			
kettle			
sheet			
toothpaste			

Other words and expressions

I'm afraid . . .
I'm being served, thanks.
What a pity.
over there
matching colours
among

on the | first / second / top | floor

in the basement
since then
originally
sold out

3 Clothes and shopping: Key

——— 1 ———————————————

a *earrings:* ears   *cap:* head
  gloves: hands   *brooch:* chest
  socks: feet   *hat:* head
  tie: neck   *boots:* feet
  belt: waist   *necklace:* neck and shoulders
  ring: finger   *scarf:* neck
  bracelet: wrist

——— 2 ———————————————

a There are a lot of possibilities. Here are some of them:

a thin cotton blouse   warm leather gloves
a long silk scarf   a thick suede jacket

——— 3 ———————————————

a Here are the three conversations:

1 Shop assistant: Can I help you?
  Customer: I'm being served, thanks.

2 Customer: Excuse me. Have you got this blouse in size 12?
  Shop assistant: No, I'm afraid we've sold out.
  Customer: Oh, what a pity.

3 Customer: Could I try on this dress?
  Shop assistant: Yes, of course. The changing-room's over there.
  Customer: *(A few minutes later)* I'm afraid it's too small.
  Shop assistant: Well, would you like to try on a bigger size?
  Customer: Yes, please.

4

a 1   a
   2   d
   3   Five, because the bones in the neck are still soft.

b There are a lot of possible answers.

c These are the irregular verbs:

Infinitive	*Past*	*Past participle*
hold	held	held
think	thought	thought
make	made	made
wear	wore	worn
go	went	gone
forget	forgot	forgotten
begin	began	begun
put	put	put

5

a You can start on the 5th floor or in the basement:

5th floor: a bed
4th floor: a cassette, a novel, a note pad
3rd floor: a tracksuit, an exercise bicycle, some underwear
2nd floor: some underwear
1st floor: two single sheets
ground floor: a tube of toothpaste, needles and thread
basement: a kettle, knives and forks

The present for Ted could be from any department.

b ▭ The additional things were:

another book
some envelopes
some toys (Jean bought these.)

SELF-STUDY ACTIVITIES

3 b) In Britain you would buy these things in these shops:

stamps: the post office
a *film:* a chemist's/photographic shop
cigarettes: a tobacconist's/sweet shop
shampoo: a chemist's
liver: a butcher's
perfume: a chemist's/department store
a *cucumber:* a greengrocer's
biscuits: a grocer's
paint: a 'do-it-yourself' (DIY) shop/hardware shop

4 **Food and drink:** Teacher's notes

1

Students usually enjoy working on these puzzles individually. Allow them five minutes and then they can compare their answers in small groups. Before going on to the second activity (in the same groups), check the pronunciation of difficult items, e.g. *pear* /peə/, *cauliflower* /kɒlɪflaʊə/, and *mushroom* /mʌʃrʊm/ or /mʌʃruːm/. For further practice (possibly in a later lesson), you could give the students a list of fruit, meat and vegetables, and ask them to rank them in order of personal preference.

2

a Remind the students that their choice of superordinate (countable or uncountable) will determine the form of the verb, i.e. singular or plural. The students can decide for themselves on the choice of *all* or *most* in the different sentences. Check and discuss the answers carefully before going on to the pair work in **b**.

c This is an optional activity.

3

a Put the students in pairs. They should be able to deduce the meaning of unknown items from their knowledge of the situation (with limited dictionary assistance), so don't preteach any items that are new to them.

b When the students have checked their answers against the listening passage, play the tape a second time and tell the students to write down what the people actually ate at the restaurant.

c This is only interesting if you know that the custom will be different in the students' own country/countries. If not, you could omit this activity.

4

a Students can complete the table in pairs with the aid of a dictionary. This will only provide a partial understanding but it will be sufficient to reduce their problems with the text. If you feel the text will still be difficult, preteach *pint*, *liver* and *acute*.

b Allow the students two or three minutes to write down their answers. They can then look back through the text to find the answers they could not remember. Go through the answers and highlight the use of the present perfect with (2) and (5). You may also wish to discuss the findings with the class. For example, are they shocked or surprised at the figures?

5

a In order to answer some of the questions the students will need to have dictionaries, but they should also be encouraged to use other members of the class to find out the meanings of unknown words. When they have finished, they can compare and discuss their answers in small groups.

SELF-STUDY ACTIVITIES

1 Check answers in the next lesson and ask the students to compare their favourite salads.
2 A small picture library is particularly suitable for younger learners, and it can be a very effective way of remembering a wide range of concrete nouns. Students could do the same thing for types of clothing, animals, household objects, and so on. They could also bring their pictures to class and teach or test each other.
3 See the comment in Unit 2, Self-study activity 1, on page 13.
4 This is quite a demanding activity and may not be of interest to all your students. Make it optional.

4 Food and drink:
Key words and expressions

Nouns		Verbs	Adjectives
lamb	salmon	smell	tasty
peas	casserole	order (a meal)	ripe
cauliflower	herbs	sneeze	rare
carrot	starter	cry	medium rare
onion	main course	chop	alcoholic
grapes	dessert	mix	harmful
strawberry	bill	pour	harmless
pepper	tip	harm	dead
cherry	hangover	die	average
pineapple	breath	average	tender (meat)
garlic	alcohol	consume	acute (illness)
melon	alcoholism	leave (= allow	
mushroom	death	to remain)	
peach	average	book (a table)	
pear	sauce		
cabbage	liver		
aubergine	pint		
nuts	consumer		
consumption	meal		
cough	menu		
	spirits		

Other words and expressions

late at night	25% (twenty-five per cent)	net weight
half a million	100g (one hundred grams)	keep (him) awake
9.1 (nine point one)	no added colour	

© Cambridge University Press 1990

26

4 Food and drink: Key

a 1 Most/All vegetables are.   4 Most/All fruit is.
2 Most/All meat has.   5 All spirits are.
3 Most/All fish is.

a The order is usually:

1 decide to go out for a meal
2 book a table
3 go to the restaurant
4 sit down
5 look at the menu
6 order the meal
7 have the starter
8 have the main course
9 have dessert
10 ask for the bill
11 pay the bill
12 give the waiter a tip
13 leave the restaurant

b 🔲 The differences are:

They didn't book a table.
They asked to move to another table.
They ordered aperitifs.

They ordered wine.
They had some coffee and brandy.
They didn't give the waiter a tip.

© Cambridge University Press 1990

──── **4** ────────────────

a

Noun	Person	Adjective	Verb
alcoholism	alcoholic	alcoholic	—
consumption	consumer	—	consume
harm	—	harmful/harmless	harm
average	—	average	average
death	the deceased/corpse/ dead body	dead	die

b 1 The danger level for women is five glasses of wine a day.
   2 The rise in alcohol consumption.
   3 The average alcohol consumption for one person in a year.
   4 The number of people in the UK dependent on alcohol.
   5 Since 1980 deaths from liver disease have doubled.
   6 25% of all men with acute diseases have alcohol-related illness.

c *432 g net* = 432 grammes net weight (i.e. excluding packet, etc.)
   keep refrigerated = You must keep it cool in a fridge.
   no added colour = The colour is completely natural.
   2 kg = 2 kilogrammes
   price per lb. £1.99 = It costs £1.99 for each pound weight.
   keep in a cool dry place = Don't let it get damp or warm.
   5.64 oz = 5.64 ounces (weight)
   net weight 75 g = The weight (excluding packaging) is 75 grammes.
   best before end June 1993 = The product will not be so good after that
      date.
   325 ml = 325 millilitres
   keep out of reach of children = It is dangerous for children.
   suitable for home freezing = It is all right to freeze this at home.

──── **5** ────────────────

a 1 coffee   5 garlic
   2 steak or beef   6 vinegar or lemon juice
   3 pepper   7 butter or ice
   4 onions   8 alcohol

SELF-STUDY ACTIVITIES

1 There are lots of answers here. Check in a dictionary.

3 Here are a few examples; there are many more:

beer bottle	beer glasses	teacup	sugar bowl
wine bottle	wine glasses	coffee cup	cereal bowl
milk bottle	whisky glasses	eggcup	soup bowl
hot water bottle	reading glasses	World Cup	washing-up bowl

5 People and relationships:
Teacher's notes

1
---

a Make sure your students understand what a prefix is before they begin this exercise. You should also allow them the use of dictionaries to look up any unknown words in the sentences. When they have finished, you can discuss their conclusions. It is important to point out that the use of *il-/ir-/im-* is partly predictable but that *un-* (by far the most common of the four prefixes) is not.

2
---

a *Nervous* is a notorious 'false friend', and at some point you should point out that its use is more restricted in English than in many other languages. As an introduction to the exercise, you could put the four words from the left-hand column on the board and ask the students to mime the meaning. In so doing, they may demonstrate some of the gestures contained in the exercise.

b This invitation invariably seems to elicit *pick my nose* amongst other possibilities!

c An optional activity which could be given as homework.

3
---

a Put the students into pairs to work out the most usual order for these events, and allow them to use dictionaries. When you check the answers, you can invite discussion on the possible variations in this order, and it is also a good opportunity to introduce the frequent use of *get + adjective/past participle* to signify a change in state (e.g. *get tired, get drunk,* and so on).

b Follow the instructions in the Student's Book and then ask for situations from the students to check their understanding. For example:

1 Why would you ignore someone?
2 What might make you jealous?
3 Tell me something that you regret.

c 〔▭〕 Play the tape and then put the students into small groups to compare their answers. If necessary, play the tape a second time.

──── **4** ──────────────────

a These useful expressions are fairly self-explanatory, but the students may not know them as fixed lexical phrases.

b Put the students into small groups for this activity.

c An optional activity which could be set as homework.

──── **5** ──────────────────

a With the help of bilingual dictionaries, the students should be able to complete this activity without your assistance, although you may need to help with pronunciation.

b The activity has been devised in this way to practise the 's genitive structure which is a common source of error. Before you put the students into pairs, explain and illustrate this structure with examples on the board.

──── **6** ──────────────────

This story permits a number of different permutations.

──── │ **SELF-STUDY ACTIVITIES** │ ──────────────────

1 Check the answers in class and ask the students to write sentences about themselves using the underlined vocabulary.
2 Check the answers in class before setting the third activity.

5 People and relationships:
Key words and expressions

Nouns	Verbs	Adjectives	
stepmother	tap	(il)legal	nervous
stepfather	bite	(il)legible	bored
stepsister	scratch	(il)literate	depressed
brother-in-law	rub	(ir)rational	pregnant
sister-in-law	fold	(ir)regular	jealous
mother-in-law	ignore	(ir)responsible	lonely
father-in-law	leave (your husband)	(im)practical	embarrassed
nephew	regret	(im)polite	miserable
niece	promise	(im)patient	cloudy
grandmother	whisper	(un)satisfactory	sunny
lips	collapse	foggy	
nails	stand up	familiar	
hips	scream	crowded	
cousin	laugh		
relationship	stare		
colleague	baby-sit		
	look after		
	be brought up		

Other words and expressions

get changed	lose (your) temper	play a trick on (her)
get married	keep a promise	beside
get engaged	keep a secret	go wrong
get divorced	break a promise	my mother's brother
get to know (her)	tell a lie	my father's sister
fall in love	tell the truth	the sun came out
have a baby	do (him) a favour	

5 People and relationships: Key

───── **1** ─────────────────────────

a The rule is that we use:
il- before the letter 'l'
ir- before the letter 'r'
im- before the letter 'p'
un- before other letters

b Examples which follow the pattern are: illogical, irrelevant, imperfect, etc.
One which doesn't is: unlucky.

───── **2** ─────────────────────────

a Different people do different things at different times but these are
possible reactions:

tap your feet   rub your neck/lips/arms
bite your lips/nails   fold your arms
scratch your head   put your hands on your hips

───── **3** ─────────────────────────

a This might be the order:

1 You meet someone.   5 You get married.
2 You get to know them.   6 You become pregnant.
3 You fall in love with them. 7 You have a baby.
4 You get engaged.   8 You get divorced.

c 1 F   2 T   3 T   4 F   5 F   6 T   7 T   8 T

───── **4** ─────────────────────────────

a There are no fixed answers here.

c Jill: Can you keep a secret?
   Joe: What is it?
   Jill: Jack and I are getting married.
   Joe: I know. To tell you the truth, Jack told me.
   Jill: Will you do me a favour?
   Joe: What is it?
   Jill: Tell Jack we're *not* getting married.

───── **6** ─────────────────────────────

a There are lots of possible stories here.

───── **SELF-STUDY ACTIVITIES** ─────────

1 a) We get on very well, but our interests/likes/dislikes are all different.
  b) I hate looking after babies while their parents are out.
  c) When I was younger I was frightened of the dark.
  d) Could you stay with the children and make sure they are all right while I go to the shops?
  e) She was born in the city but she spent her childhood on a farm.

2 The opposites are:

  fat – thin
  curly hair – straight hair
  broad shoulders – narrow shoulders
  black hair – blonde hair
  dark skin – fair skin

6 Revision and expansion:
Teacher's notes

1

The purpose of this activity is not that the students should produce identical answers. They may decide on three, four, or even five groups, and the contents of each of the groups may certainly vary. What is important is that the organising principles adopted are meaningful to each individual student. When they have finished, they can compare their groups and explain the rationale for their decisions.

2

The students could create their own exercise of this type. Tell them to think of six more pairs of opposites or synonyms. They can then write the words in a box in a jumbled order, and test other students in the class.

3

For the second part of the exercise, you could divide the class into groups of three, instead of pairs. Each student in a group takes responsibility for about five items, which they must then explain to the other members of the group. Encourage the students to discuss the methods being used; are they the best way to explain the meaning in each case?

4

---

a Some of the vocabulary in this exercise is being included for the first time so students may require some help. Initially, though, see if they can deduce the meaning (individually or in pairs), and then discuss the answers with the class.

b Most of the replies require a verbal response, however brief, and even in situations which do not require a spoken answer, some form of acknowledgement would be necessary, e.g. a smile. When the students have completed their replies, check the answers before putting them into pairs to practise the dialogues.

—— **5** ————————————————————————

If the students cannot complete the exercise from memory, tell them to look back through the units to try and find the answers.

—— **6** ————————————————————————

Depending on the nationality of your students, some of these mistakes will be more relevant than others. If you are teaching a monolingual group, you may want to look through the units and write your own sentences based on the type of mistakes your students are most likely to make.

—— **7** ————————————————————————

Encourage the students to be as imaginative as they wish, but remind them that they cannot just offer two words – they must explain the connection or give example sentences.

—— **8** ————————————————————————

The second part could be done as a class game. Each student must think of one example and define it for the rest of the class. After the definitions, the other students must write down the name of the object being defined. The winner is the student who has correctly identified the most objects.

—— **9** ————————————————————————

This is an enjoyable way of revising a familiar lexical area but from a slightly different perspective.

—— **10** ————————————————————————

This exercise revises verbs from the units but with new information, i.e. the choice of infinitive or gerund following the verb.

—— **11** ————————————————————————

When this table is finally completed the students will have their own personal record of irregular verb patterns. At this stage, tell them not to guess at answers, or worry about the verbs they have not yet encountered. Ask them to fill in what they know, and then at regular intervals throughout the book you can return to this table and tell the students to add any irregular forms they have recently learned.

6 Revision and expansion:
New words and expressions

Nouns	Adjectives	Verbs	Expressions
pullover	asleep	get (= fetch)	Help yourself.
jumper	rude	refuse	Never mind.
cutlery		skid	Don't worry.
vehicle		kick	Have you got a light?
			Go ahead.

VERB + infinitive, e.g. promise, refuse,
want, offer, decide

VERB + gerund, e.g. love, enjoy, don't
mind, dislike, can't stand

Expressions continued:
That's all, thanks.
Anything else?
Could I leave a message?
(I'm) in a hurry.
Could you give me a hand?
Do you mind if I . . .?

6 Revision and expansion: Key

There is no fixed answer here but you should be able to explain your grouping of the words and phrases.

───── **2** ─────

The opposites are:

full – empty
optimistic – pessimistic
dirty – clean
awake – asleep
lazy – hard-working
thin – thick

The synonyms are:

jumper – pullover
go on – continue
choose – select
wait a minute – hang on
rude – impolite
awful – terrible

───── **3** ─────

Different people will have different answers but here are some possible ones:

1 Demonstration or gesture: bite, pregnant, pour, laugh, frighten
2 Synonym or opposite: dirty, awake, shy
3 Giving examples: cutlery, do someone a favour, spirits
4 Definition or explanation: a sink, pregnant, do someone a favour, medium rare
5 Situation: pregnant, laugh, shy, frighten, do someone a favour, embarrassed

—— **4** ——————————————————

a and **b**

1 A: Can I help you?
   B: I'm being served, thanks.
   A: *(No answer necessary)*

2 A: Anything else?
   B: No, that's all, thanks.
   A: Right. That'll be £3.80, please.

3 A: Sorry I'm late.
   B: Never mind, don't worry.
   A: *(No answer necessary)*

4 A: What's the matter?
   B: Nothing. Why?
   A: Well, . . . *(many possibilities)*

5 A: Could I leave a message?
   B: Yeah, sure. I'll just get a pen.
   A: Thanks.

6 A: Have you got a light?
   B: Sorry, I don't smoke.
   A: Oh, OK.

7 A: Do you mind if I smoke?
   B: No, go ahead.
   A: Thanks.

8 A: Could you give me a hand?
   B: Sorry. I'm in a hurry.
   A: Oh, OK.

9 A: Could I borrow your pen?
   B: Yes, help yourself.
   A: Thank you.

—— **5** ——————————————————

Here are some possible answers:

a secret
a diary—(KEEP)— a promise
a record

a mistake
a mess —(MAKE)—the bed
a decision

married
dressed —(GET)— divorced
changed

—— **6** ————————————————

The correct sentences are:

1 What does *improve* mean?
2 How is it written?
3 Don't turn the tap on.
4 It's a thing for making coffee.
5 I never wear earrings.
6 Would you like to try on a bigger size?
7 Don't leave the meat in the oven too long.
8 The meal wasn't very good but the first course was nice.
9 I want to get to know English people.
10 Have you got / Do you have a light?

—— **7** ————————————————

There are lots of answers but you must explain the connections.

—— **9** ————————————————

Here are some examples:

Green food	*Red food*	*Yellow food*	*White food*
beans	raspberries	grapefruit	flour
lettuces	radishes	maize/corn	celery
cabbages	tomatoes	peaches	rice

—— **10** ————————————————

refuse *to* . . .	can't stand . . . *-ing*
want *to* . . .	love . . . *-ing*
offer *to* . . .	don't mind . . . *-ing*
promise *to* . . .	dislike . . . *-ing*

7 Time: Teacher's notes

Time expressions are a common source of error for most nationalities, and at the end of the activity you could ask your students to identify the errors which they are most likely to make as a result of interference from their first language.

——— 2 ———————————————————————

The permutations are endless here, so it may be advisable to restrict the number of expressions to about twelve per student.

——— 3 ———————————————————————

a With a multilingual group this exercise often generates a lot of discussion; different nationalities seem to have quite different ideas about, for example, the beginning of adulthood. The age of the students can also influence their perception of middle age and old age.

Before they discuss their answers, point out the constructions at the end of **a** in order to avoid the potential error '. . . begins at 18 *years*'. It is also important that the students are familiar with the verb *last* in this context.

b Put the students in groups of three or four and allow them to use dictionaries to look up unknown words.

——— 4 ———————————————————————

a The students will need to look at the definitions carefully so this part of the exercise is best done individually. When you check their answers, point out that *have a good time* permits different adjectives, e.g. 'have a *great/fantastic/terrible* time'. For this question it would also be acceptable to say 'had the time of our lives'.

Put the students into pairs to practise the dialogues. Afterwards they could prepare their own dialogues using these time expressions, or write sentences about themselves. For example:

I usually get to school on time.
I had a great time at the disco last night.

b All of these replies from B would require some kind of acknowledgement from A, either to register pleasure or simply understanding. In these examples, 'I see' or 'Oh, good' would seem to be the most likely and appropriate, and it is important that students become proficient in the use of these common expressions in spoken exchanges; without them they may sound rude or indifferent.

5

a The focus of this activity (as with several activities in this unit) is not so much on vocabulary which is unfamiliar to the students, as on vocabulary which is either used incorrectly by students, e.g. 'I'm afraid *but* he's out', or vocabulary which students at this level rarely seem to activate, e.g. '*I'll be back* in half an hour'. When the students have managed to separate the two conversations, you may need to highlight the use of some of these expressions with further examples.

At this stage the students could learn 'I'll be expecting you' as a fixed expression in a particular context, without any particular reference to the future continuous (with which they will not be familiar).

b This activity is likely to be more successful if you provide the students with brief role-cards. For example:

A: You are phoning Maria. You want some help with some homework you have to finish by tomorrow. It is now 5 p.m. and you are going out at 7.30 p.m.	**B:** You live with Maria. She's gone to a friend's but you are expecting her back for dinner at about 7 p.m. It is now 5 p.m.

Give each student a minute to digest the information on the role card and then let them act out the situations in pairs.

SELF-STUDY ACTIVITIES

1 See the comment in Unit 2, Self-study activity 1, on page 13.
2 Many vocabulary problems stem from the variety of ways in which common words can be used. *Time* is a good example, but you could easily construct similar exercises on other words which may not have a single translation equivalent in the students' mother tongue, e.g. *place* (noun), *take* (verb), *light* (adj.), *by* (prep. and adv.).

7 **Time:** Key words and expressions

Nouns	Verbs	Adverbs	Prepositions
adolescent	last	occasionally	at (3 o'clock)
adolescence	retire	almost	on (Friday)
teenager	worry (about it)	recently	in (January, 1976)
youth	ring (her) back	just (after	before (leaving)
adult	be back	10 o'clock)	after (leaving)
pensioner		just (over a	for (three weeks)
childhood		month ago)	since (last week,
middle age			1986, Monday)
old age			
departure			
time			

Other words and expressions

How about (tomorrow)?
What time shall we meet?
I wonder if I could (see you)?
That would be great.
Any idea when (she'll arrive)?
I'm expecting (a phone call).
I'll be expecting you.
go bald
lose weight
put on weight
get drunk
get into trouble
have a good time

Telephone language

This is (Donald).
Could I speak to (Tim)?
I'm afraid he's out.
Do you know when
  (she)'ll be back?

Adjectives

middle-aged
elderly
punctual
convenient
urgent

Time expressions

this evening	in time
yesterday evening	from time to time
next week/month	for a while
last night/week	for the time being
tonight	in the last few days
on time	

7 Time: Key

1

a
1. How long are you staying?
2. I saw him *last* night. (or *yesterday evening*)
3. I didn't sleep very well *last* night.
4. I haven't seen her *for* three weeks.
5. What are you doing *tonight*? (or *this evening*)
6. When did you arrive *in* London?
7. I arrived two days *ago*.
8. What time shall we meet?
9. I'm going there next month.
10. Before *leaving* we must get some souvenirs.
11. I haven't seen her in the last *few* days. (or *recently*)
12. I'm going to the shop but I'll be back *in* half an hour.

2

a There are a lot of possible answers.

3

a Most British people would answer something like this:

baby = 0 to 2 (approximately)
child = 2 to 12 (approximately)
teenager = 13 to 19
youth = 13 to 18 (approximately)
adolescent = 14 to 17 (approximately)
adult = 16/18 upwards
pensioner = after 60 or 65 usually
middle age = between 35 and 60 (depending on *your* age)
old age = after 70 (approximately – depending on *your* age)
elderly = after 70 (approximately – depending on *your* age)

b There will be different opinions on this.

—— 4 ——

a 1 from time to time
2 on time
3 had a great time / had the time of our lives
4 for the time being
5 in good time

b Here are some possible answers:

1 I thought so.　　3 Oh, good.　5 Oh, good.
2 Maybe he's got lost.　4 I see.

—— 5 ——

a One conversation goes like this:

A: Hello. Could I speak to Jeremy, please?
B: I'm afraid he's out at the moment.
A: Oh dear. Any idea when he'll be back?
B: Well, I'm expecting him in time for dinner.
A: Not till then?
B: About then. Shall I ask him to ring you back?
A: No. Don't worry. I'll give him a ring later.

The other one goes like this:

A: Hello, Maurice. This is Donald.
B: Oh, hello.
A: Look, I wonder if I could see you some time soon.
B: Yeah, sure. Is the day after tomorrow convenient?
A: Can't you make it earlier?
B: Well, if it's urgent, how about right now?
A: Yeah, that would be great! I'll be there in twenty minutes.
B: OK. I'll be expecting you.

——| SELF-STUDY ACTIVITIES |——

1 Here are some examples:

bedtime　　　time lag
half time　　time signal
summertime

8 Holidays and travel: Teacher's notes

a Before the students begin this exercise, you may wish to teach the pronunciation of certain items, e.g. *lounge* /laʊndʒ/, *resort* /rɪzɔːt/, and *excess baggage* /ekses bægɪdʒ/. They can then work on the exercise in pairs, using a dictionary where necessary.

b This part does permit some variation. For example, there is no reason why *holiday resort* cannot go before or after *charter flight*. The students may require your help with the construction of some of their sentences, and this is also an opportunity to check some important verbs, e.g. *book* (a flight), *get on* (a plane).

──── 2 ────────────────

Before the students complete the exercise, make sure they are clear on the difference between countable and uncountable nouns. There is an explanation on page 93 in the Student's Book.

──── 3 ────────────────

a If the students do not have dictionaries, you could write the answers on the board in a jumbled list.

b ▭ Play the tape to the class stopping after each question so that you can practise the pronunciation of the items in complete sentences (most of these adjectives have pronunciation difficulties for the student). The second time you play the tape you can ask individual students to provide a suitable reply.

c Put the students in pairs to complete the dialogue and practise it.

──── 4 ────────────────

a This activity is best done in small groups.

46

b Make sure the students do not look at the text before they have discussed their answers to the questions.

c The use of synonymy to avoid the repetition of an item of vocabulary is a common feature of texts. Students should be aware of this feature as it can often help them to deduce the meaning of unknown items in a text.

——— 5 ———————————————————

a If the students find this part very easy, you could expand the new input by introducing some adjectival derivatives, e.g. *rocky, mountainous,* and *touristy* (*touristic* being a common student error). These items could be incorporated in their postcards just as easily. With the existing words, though, you will need to check the pronunciation of *yacht* /jɒt/ and *sunbathe* /sʌnbeɪð/.

b This makes a very suitable homework activity.

——— | SELF-STUDY ACTIVITIES | ———————————

1 These words are a notorious source of confusion so you will need to check the answers in class carefully and clarify any difficulties the students may have had. One point you should mention is that *travel* is not usually used as a countable noun in English as in many other languages.

8 Holidays and travel:
Key words and expressions

Nouns

			Adjectives
departure lounge	skiing	yacht	boiling
excess baggage	sightseeing	countryside	freezing
check-in desk	enquiry	harbour	awful
boarding card	strike	beach	filthy
holiday resort	information	rocks	ancient
traveller's cheques	luggage	sand	exhausted
travel agency	advice	coastline	tiring
charter flight	news	lake	delicious
camping	valley	mountain	enormous
stewardess			favourite
view			foreign
tour			tiny

Other words and expressions

once a (year)	take a holiday	sunbathe
twice a (week)	go away	prefer (this to that)
go abroad	can't afford (it)	on television
head for		

8 Holidays and travel: Key

1
---

a departure lounge   holiday resort
excess baggage   charter flight
boarding card   traveller's cheques
check-in desk   travel agency

b The correct order depends on the sentences you write. One possible answer is:

1 First of all we went to a *travel agency* to get some information.
2 We decided to go to a *holiday resort* abroad.
3 We bought tickets for a *charter flight*.
4 Later we went to the bank and got some *traveller's cheques*.
5 At the airport we took our luggage to the *check-in desk*.
6 Our bags were quite heavy but we didn't have to pay *excess baggage*.
7 We had to wait for about half an hour in the *departure lounge*.
8 Finally, they called our flight and I showed the stewardess my *boarding card* as I got on the plane.

2
---

a 1 information   5 a lot of snow
2 luggage   6 some
3 enquiries   7 tours
4 resorts   8 some

3
---

a 2 big   6 cold
3 nice   7 bad
4 small   8 dirty
5 tired   9 old
           10 good

≫→

b ⬚

  3 Yeah, it was very big.
  4 Yeah, it was very dirty.
  5 Yeah, it was very small.
  6 Yeah, it was very old.
  7 Yeah, it wasn't very good.
  8 Yeah, we were very tired.

c 1 ancient   5 filthy
      2 tiny   6 freezing
      3 delicious   7 boiling
      4 awful   8 exhausted

4

c 1 favourite   4 go to
      2 abroad   5 go away
      3 the seaside 6 preferred to

5

a 1 The beach scene: coastline, tourists, beach, sunbathe, rocks, sand, view
      2 The harbour scene: yacht, tourists, harbour, view
      3 The mountain scene: valley, mountains, countryside, snow, lake, view

SELF-STUDY ACTIVITIES

1 a) tour/trip
   b) trip
   c) journey/trip
   d) cruise
   e) trip
   f) journey

3 a) A single room has one bed for one person.
    A double room has one bed for two people.
    Twin beds are two single beds.
  b) Bed and breakfast provides a bed for the night and breakfast only.
    Half board also includes one other meal – lunch or dinner.
    Full board includes all your meals.
  c) A fare is paid for transport.
    A bill is paid for goods or services.

9 Transport: Teacher's notes

1

a 📼 When you have played the tape once, the students can compare their answers with a partner. You can discuss any differences of opinion before playing the tape a second time. Stop the tape as you go through and highlight the use of new expressions, e.g. *keep* + *gerund*, *get* (= reach or arrive), *halfway along*, etc.

2

a This should be revision for most students. If so, you could extend the activity by asking them to think of other verbs with these endings, i.e. *-ide*, *-ive*, *-ch*, and *-ake*, which have a similar pattern, and those which are different. They could use the Irregular Verb list at the back of their books to check.

b Students are often surprised to learn that you can *get on* a train but not a car, and that you *ride* a motorbike (in English).

c This could be set as homework.

3

a Students could do the first part individually or in pairs. When you check their answers, highlight the pronunciation of *buffet* /bʊfeɪ/, and this very common use of *get* (= obtain/acquire).

b Pairs practice.

c Optional.

4

a The first part is very straightforward and the students should be able to work out the meaning of unknown words by a process of deduction and elimination.

b Although there may be several new items of vocabulary in these sentences, e.g. *messenger* and *package*, allow the students to use dictionaries to find out the meaning for themselves. Tell the students that they should be prepared to give reasons for their choice in each case.

5

a This is deceptively difficult so allow the students at least ten minutes to work out the correct answer. They can then compare their answers in pairs or small groups (students who have been unable to complete the exercise can now enlist the help of their colleagues). The same pairs or groups can also work together on **b**.

SELF-STUDY ACTIVITIES

3 Being aware of American English equivalents for British English words is particularly relevant to students from E. Asia and S. America who usually encounter more American English than British English. If you work in these areas, you may wish to include more exercises of this type throughout the course. Certainly you can expect a good monolingual dictionary to refer to the existence of alternative forms; these are usually indicated by 'US' or 'AmE', and 'GB' or 'BrE'.

9 **Transport:** Key words and expressions

Nouns	Verbs	Giving directions
roundabout	get into (a car)	turn right/left into . . .
main road	get out of (a car)	take the first/second (turning)
traffic lights	get on (a bus)	on the left/right (hand side)
motorbike	get off (a bus)	keep going . . .
coach	get/have (a lift)	until you get to . . .
buffet car	take (a taxi)	just before/after . . .
platform	ride (a horse)	
sports car	catch (a bus)	
van	miss (a bus)	
ambulance	knock (him) down	
lorry	deliver	
tractor	swerve	
camper	crash (into it)	
rowing boat	damage	
pedestrian crossing	injure	
roundabout	change (trains)	
messenger	brake	
package	keep fit	
sleeper		
ticket office		
lost property		
chemist		

Other words and expressions

learn how to do something	move house	make a reservation
single	parked cars	slightly (damaged)
return	close (to it)	badly (damaged)

© Cambridge University Press 1990

9 Transport: Key

a 📼 The map should look like this when you have finished:

①= the bus stop   ③= the underground station
②= the bank   ④= the restaurant

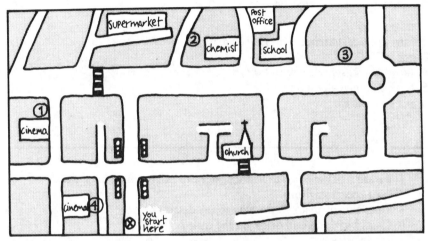

b These are possible sets of directions:

1 Now you are outside the restaurant. Go back down this road, turn right and then turn left at the traffic lights. When you come to the main road, turn left and then turn right just after the pedestrian crossing. Take the first road on your right and you will see the supermarket on your left.
2 Now you are outside the supermarket. Go back down this road and turn left. When you come to the main road, turn left and then take the second road on your left. The post office is on the right, almost opposite the chemist.

2

a

Infinitive	Past tense	Past participle
to get	got	got
to ride	rode	ridden
to drive	drove	driven
to take	took	taken
to catch	caught	caught

b The *wrong* answers are:

1 a car   2 a car   3 a motorbike   4 a bike   5 a taxi

c The most natural answers are:

1 take a taxi
2 (any correct sentence with *ride* or *drive*)
3 got on
4 (any correct sentence with *take*)
5 took a plane/caught a plane
6 got into the car

3

a 1 I want a ticket to go to Manchester but not to come back again.
2 (at a coach station)
3 Does this train go all the way to my destination?
4 Can I buy food and drink on the train?
5 (at an airport)
6 Where is the place in the station to buy tickets?
7 How much is a ticket to go to Glasgow and come back again?
8 (probably on the underground)
9 Exactly where in the station do I get on the train?
10 Can I get a train to Edinburgh with a special place to sleep during the journey?
11 I am looking for the office where they keep things that people have lost in the station or on the train.
12 Do I need to pay for a special ticket with a seat number or will there be enough places on the train for everyone to sit down?

4
---

a
1	a sports car	8	a taxi
2	an ambulance	9	a coach
3	a Mercedes	10	a bike
4	a bus	11	a motorbike
5	a horse	12	a camper
6	a tractor	13	a van
7	a Jeep		

b You might not agree with all of these:

1 tractor, horse, Jeep
2 motorbike, bike
3 sports car, Mercedes
4 bus, taxi
5 camper, motorbike, sports car
6 ambulance
7 van
8 bike

5
---

a The order of the sentences is: 6, 2, 4, 1, 5, 3.

b Whose fault was the accident? Possible answers are: the lorry driver; the car driver; the van driver.

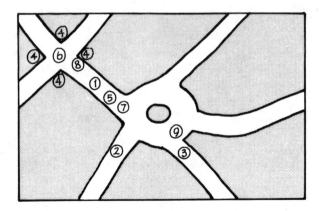

© Cambridge University Press 1990

SELF-STUDY ACTIVITIES

3 *British English*   *American English*

a) underground   subway
b) lorry   truck
c) taxi   cab
d) lift   elevator
e) pavement   sidewalk
f) petrol station gas station
g) return ticket   round trip ticket
h) motorway   highway

4

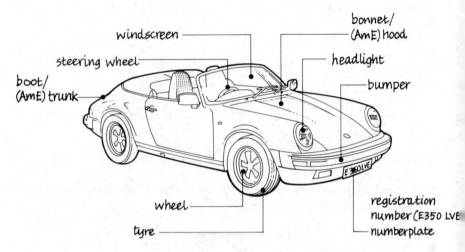

10 Work: Teacher's notes

—— 1 ——

a Grids are another easy and efficient way of recording and storing new vocabulary. (For another example see Self-study activity 1 in Unit 15.)

While the students are completing the grid, go round the class and help with any problems they may be having, e.g. farmers *grow food*, *cultivate land* and *breed animals* – your students may be trying to express one or all of these *duties*.

When they have completed what they can and compared their answers with a partner, go through the answers with the class. This is a good opportunity to point out one clear case of versatility in English, namely the ability of many word forms to function in different word classes. In this case your students may not realise that *farm* and *model* can both function as verbs to define the activities of farmers and models.

b Begin by illustrating the pattern, e.g.:

A: What do you call a person who (designs houses)?
B: An architect.

The students can then practise in pairs.

—— 2 ——

Begin by explaining any new words on the dials; *skilled* and *stressful* are likely to cause the most difficulty. Put the students into groups of four or five and explain the rules of the game carefully (see instructions in Student's Book).

—— 3 ——

a If the first exercise proves very easy, you could extend the lexical set with the addition of derivatives, i.e. *application (form)*, *acceptance*, *promote*, *advertising*, and so on.

b 🔲 The students are being asked to transfer quite a lot of information from the listening passage to the grid in their books. One way to reduce the load is to divide the task between two students, i.e. one student fills in the left-hand column while a partner completes the other. They can then exchange their information in pairs before listening to the tape a second time to confirm each other's answers. At the end you could extend the activity by asking the pairs to discuss other reasons for giving up a job.

4

a When the students have completed the first task, ask them to write down the translation equivalent for *keep* in each of these sentences. If they require a number of different verbs, then *keep* is clearly a word requiring a lot of attention.

b This provides further practice of different uses of *keep* and could be done in small groups. The students need not be confined to the list given in the book – encourage them to add their own ideas. If the students have no previous work experience, we would advise you to omit this activity.

5

The students should not merely write down the most appropriate job for each person, they should also be able to give reasons for their choice with reference to the text. To ensure this happens, tell them to underline or write down the words and phrases in the text which lead them to their final decision.

If you think your students will be overwhelmed or distracted by the amount of new vocabulary in the text, preteach some of the important items. Try and keep this to a minimum, otherwise the problem-solving aspect will be reduced and some of the fun will be lost.

SELF-STUDY ACTIVITIES

1 The students could compare their answers to this activity in a future lesson.
2 This type of activity can be extended in different ways. For example, ask the students to write down ten items they might see on a teacher's desk, eight items they might see on a bank manager's desk, and eight items they might see on a journalist's desk. Some items may be common to all three, but encourage them to think of the differences.

10 Work: Key words and expressions

Occupations	Other nouns	Verbs	Adjectives	
mechanic	articles	fix	boring	organised
dentist	advert	look after	exciting	efficient
lawyer	client	treat	creative	sociable
model	diary	model	stressful	quiet
farmer	appointment	cultivate	well-paid	polite
photographer	record	grow	skilled	reliable
journalist	qualifications	report	unskilled	clever
architect	experience	design	badly paid	tidy
accountant	abilities	deal with	professional	
carpenter		accept	unpleasant	
traffic warden		keep		
		sack		

Places of work   represent

surgery   farm
court   factory
studio

Other words and expressions

get promotion
apply for (a job)
be satisfied with (a person/thing)
give (a person) an interview
offer (a person) a job
get to (work)

on time
answer a letter
make a phone call
receive a phone call
get angry with (a person)

10 **Work:** Key

───── **1** ─────────────────────────────

a

Job	Place of work	Duties
1 mechanic	garage	repairs your car
2 secretary	office	does general office work
3 dentist	surgery	looks after your teeth
4 lawyer	court or office	advises and represents people
5 model	studio	poses for photos or paintings
6 farmer	farm	looks after the farm, animals and crops
7 photographer	studio	takes photographs
8 journalist	office	writes articles
9 architect	office	designs houses
10 accountant	office	looks after the accounts

───── **2** ─────────────────────────────

a There are a lot of possible answers here.

───── **3** ─────────────────────────────

a Here is the probable order:

1 She saw the advert.
2 She applied for the job.
3 They gave her an interview.
4 They offered her the job.
5 She accepted the job.
6 She got promotion.
7 They weren't satisfied with her work.
8 They sacked her.

© Cambridge University Press 1990

62

b 📼 The facts about the two jobs are as follows (you could have selected any four from each list):

Present job	*New job*
in charge of a small team	contact with engineers, builders, etc.
a lot of responsibility	a lot of travelling locally
desk job/paperwork	a lower salary
little chance of promotion	good promotion prospects
a small company	part of a new project

—— 4

a 1) 6; 2) 3; 3) 13; 4) 3

b The answer depends on you.

—— 5

There are several possibilities here: one is that Sheila should apply for the first job, Alice for the second and Jake for the third.

SELF-STUDY ACTIVITIES

3 inefficient; unreliable; impolite; disorganised; unpleasant; untidy; unsociable; unfriendly.

11 **Crime:** Teacher's notes

―――― **1** ――――――――――――――――

This is another example of a vocabulary network for the students to complete with the help of dictionaries. As the students will encounter some of the items later on in the unit, you could leave this exercise until the end, and then use it for consolidation and revision.

―――― **2** ――――――――――――――――

a The first part of the exercise should be done in groups. You may have to preteach *average* and *arrest* (and *burgle* if you have omitted the first exercise).

b If the students are particularly surprised and/or interested by the findings in the text, they could form groups and discuss the information. Why, for example, do burglars live quite near the houses they burgle?

c You will need to point out that these synonyms are not interchangeable in every context (e.g. you cannot talk about an *unoccupied* bottle).

d Give the students five minutes to complete the first five sentences and then add three more ideas of their own. They can do this individually but should be allowed to use dictionaries. Check their answers and then put them into groups for the discussion activity **e**.

―――― **3** ――――――――――――――――

a Also ideal for small groups, although some students prefer to work out the order on their own and then compare their answer with other students. It should not be necessary to preteach any items of vocabulary; the students either deduce the meaning from context or use their dictionaries to look up new words, e.g. *stocking, number plate, shotgun, shoot, rush out, hand over.*

4

Although bilingual dictionaries are frowned upon by some language teachers, we believe that a good bilingual dictionary is a very valuable resource, and one that students use without fear or hesitation. As such, we would prefer to make students aware of the strengths and limitations of these dictionaries, rather than see them used badly in a clandestine way.

When the students attempt the first exercise, it may be a sensible precaution to make them cover the newspaper text. When the students have compared answers, you could write their different choices on the board. It is particularly interesting to do this if your students are working from different dictionaries.

We have tried to cover the likely right and wrong answers given by the dictionaries but you may still be called upon to adjudicate on possible answers.

5

a Make sure the students understand *smuggler* and *illegal* before they read the text. You could also use the introductory discussion to teach one or two new items in the text. However, this should be kept to a minimum, otherwise the text will begin to lose any fascination. Make sure the students underline all the information which is new to them.

b One of the most important items of vocabulary in the text is *realise*, and this activity provides a very natural way of using the item. However, it will not be easy for the students to use the verb naturally and appropriately (unless they are very familiar with it already), so don't worry if they are not exploiting the item as much as you would wish.

SELF-STUDY ACTIVITIES

1 One of the virtues of vocabulary networks is that they can be expanded in all sorts of imaginative ways. As part of your classwork, you could ask the students to add *kidnapping* and *investigate* to the network they completed in Exercise 1 of the unit, and then, as a self-study activity, you could tell them to add a further six items. In your next lesson the students could compare their networks to see how differently they have been developed.

2 This activity can also be used as the basis for a future classwork activity. Check their answers in class and then put them into pairs to think of more examples of serious crime, terrorist attack, dangerous weapons, types of death penalty, and crimes which are normally punishable by means of a fine.

11 **Crime:** Key words and expressions

Nouns	Verbs	Adjectives	Other words and expressions
burglar alarm	take (time)	injured	
lock	take place	illegal	at night
bolt	arrest	guilty	within (a mile) of
stocking	investigate	nervous	a bomb went off
terrorist	search	relaxed	a bomb exploded
damage	catch		
number plate	occur		
shotgun	install		
warning	set off (an alarm)		**Person, crime and verb**
explosive	rush (in/out)		criminal – crime – commit (a crime)
location	shoot (a person)		burglar – burglary – burgle
injuries	evacuate		murderer – murder – murder
hijacking	plant (a bomb)		rapist – rape – rape
customs	behave		robber – robbery – rob
customs	attack		mugger – mugging – mug
official	feel (nervous)		thief – theft – steal
conveyor belt	look (nervous)		smuggler – smuggling – smuggle
	warn		

© Cambridge University Press 1990

11 Crime: Key

a

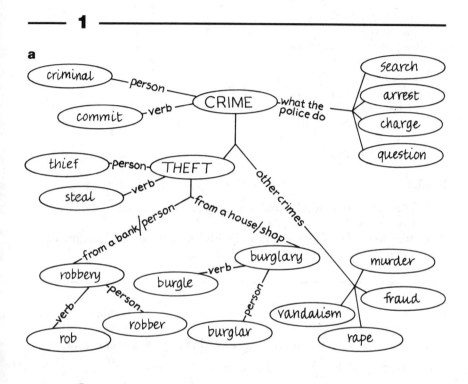

a and **b** 1 F   2 T   3 T   4 T   5 F   6 T   7 T

c 1 within a mile or two of
    2 one chance in 25
    3 unoccupied
    4 Most burglars are never caught.
    5 occur

d 1 alarm   4 neighbours; police
    2 locks   5 light
    3 key

© Cambridge University Press 1990

3

a One possible answer is:

1 You steal a car.
2 You change the number plates.
3 You drive to the bank.
4 You put stockings over your heads.
5 One person waits in the car.
6 You go in.
7 You get out your shotguns.
8 You make the customers lie on the floor.
9 The bank clerk hands over the money.
10 Someone sets off the alarm.
11 You rush out.
12 The police arrive.

b

1 The main differences are that they shot someone and they didn't get any money.
2 Both were of medium height, probably between 20 and 30 years old and they had stockings pulled over their heads.

4

a 1 exploded   2 hurt/injured   3 damage   4 warning   5 evacuate

c There are several possible answers for each, but here are some examples:

1 explosive   2 bomb   3 location   4 planted   5 injuries

SELF-STUDY ACTIVITIES

1 The police *investigate*; *kidnapping* is another type of crime.
2 death penalty – electric chair
serious crime – rape
dangerous weapon – a gun
parking fine – £50
prison sentence – five years
terrorist attack – a hijacking

12 Revision and expansion:
Teacher's notes

─── **1** ───

There is more than one correct answer for some of the compounds, e.g. *parking space* or *parking meter*. This is intentional, as it encourages the students to generate more and more vocabulary out of the activity.

When the students have organised the vocabulary into groups, they could then extend each group with more examples.

─── **2** ───

Essay and *novel* are being included here for the first time, so the students may need to use dictionaries. At the end you can discuss the different answers.

─── **3** ───

This is a similar activity to exercise 4 in Unit 6, the previous revision and expansion unit. Follow the same procedure.

─── **4** ───

This is an ideal activity for small groups. It draws on vocabulary from Unit 9, but it could easily generate new vocabulary from the students. You may need to explain *overtake*, as it is being included in the book for the first time.

─── **5** ───

Just is a very high frequency item, and it is often neglected in coursebooks. The students will already have seen it used on several occasions in this book, but this exercise provides a specific focus on its different uses. You could find more examples from a coursebook and ask the students to explain the meaning of *just* in each case.

—— 6 ————————————————————

This is an opportunity to expand the range of collocations with three very important verbs.

—— 7 ————————————————————

See the comment on a similar activity in Unit 6, exercise 6.

—— 8 ————————————————————

a Start by giving examples of the structure you want the students to practise, e.g.:
  What do you call a person who teaches?
  What do you call a person who acts in films?
The students can then test each other on the different jobs using the above pattern. When they have completed the jobs in the exercise, encourage them to think of some more examples.

b Use the same procedure but a different pattern, e.g. 'Can you think of an adjective which means very tired?' and so on.

—— 9 ————————————————————

Put the students in pairs or small groups for this activity. Allow them a few minutes to try and establish a rule for the first examples, and then discuss the answers. You could follow the same procedure for the second and third parts of the exercise.

—— 10 ————————————————————

This is similar to exercise 7 in Unit 6, the previous revision and expansion unit. Follow the same procedure.

—— 11 ————————————————————

If your students have not yet completed the Irregular Verbs table on page 103, now is the time to do so (using a dictionary to check their answers if necessary). They can then work in pairs and test each other.

—— **12** ——————————————————————————

a It is probably more effective if you illustrate the two suffixes (with examples) on the board before asking the students to do the activity in the Student's Book, i.e. identify the word class associated with the suffixes in the box.

b Check the answers to **a** before setting this second activity.

c Now refer the students to the Word building tables at the back of their books. They can check their answers and find more examples. There are several more activities using these tables in Unit 18, but having alerted the students to this feature in their books, you could make regular use of it for homework or class revision.

12 Revision and expansion:
New words and expressions

Nouns	Place expressions	Other words and expressions
essay	at (the bus stop)	at the moment
novelist	on (the table)	on the phone
indicator	in (the cupboard)	annoyed
van driver	at the end	just round the corner
bookkeeper	on the way	That's fine.
machine	in the middle	How long does it take?
operator		Have you got the time?
bank manager		You're welcome.
football player		
computer		
programmer		
opera singer		
weapon		
filing cabinet		
counterfoil		
hostage		

12 Revision and expansion: Key

Here are fifteen possible compound nouns:

traffic *lights*   *travel* agent   *buffet* car
return ticket   driving *licence*   *boarding* card
pedestrian *crossing*   *charter* flight   lost *property*
excess baggage   *bus* station   *speed* limit
parking ticket   *departure* lounge   *conveyor* belt

--- 2 ---

a 1 a cheque: anyone, in a shop, to pay for something
an article: a journalist, in a hotel, it's his/her job
an essay: a student, in a library, the teacher wants it
a novel: a novelist, at home, for pleasure or money

2 tyres and brakes: a mechanic, in a garage, for safety
passports: passport officer, at the airport, for security
answers: a teacher, in class, to see if you understand
their change: anyone, in a shop, to see that it's right

3 an application form: anyone, at home, to apply for a job
gaps: a student, in a test, to try and pass the test
a questionnaire: anyone, in the street, someone asked them to
a counterfoil: anyone, in a shop, to remember what you have paid and where

--- 3 ---

a and **b**
2 B: Oh, that's OK.   A: (*No answer necessary*)
3 B: Number seven.   A: Thanks.
4 B: I'm afraid I don't know.   A: Oh, OK.
5 B: No, I'm afraid I haven't.   A: Oh, OK.
6 B: Yes, that's fine.   A: Oh, good.
7 B: No, just round the corner.   A: Thanks.
8 B: About twenty minutes.   A: Thanks.

4

The following are examples:

1 On a pedestrian crossing, near a junction, on a double yellow line
2 On a bend, near a pedestrian crossing, near the top of a hill
3 Look in the mirror, signal, move to the centre of the road
4 Check your tyre pressure, the water in your radiator and battery
5 To turn left or right, to overtake, to pull in to the side of the road
6 In heavy rain, in fog, in tunnels

5

1) 4;   2) 3;   3) 2;   4) 1

6

7

1 I arrived two days *ago*.
2 We *spent* three days in Rome.
3 The man *checked/inspected* our passports.
4 I want *some* information.
5 *Get off* the bus.
6 I'm sorry I'm late but I *missed* the bus.
7 I don't have a *job*.
8 It's very *stressful*.
9 He *committed* a crime.
10 She *robbed* me.

8

a a van driver   a bookkeeper   a machine operator   a photographer
a bank manager   a football player   a farmer
a computer programmer   an opera singer

b *very small:* tiny
very big: huge/enormous
very dirty: filthy
very cold: freezing

9

a Some approximate answers are:

1 *at* is used with a point of time
2 *on* is used with a day/date/part of a day, e.g. Friday morning
3 *in* is used with a period of time
4 *at* is used with an exact place (a point in space)
5 *on* is used with a surface
6 *in* is used with three-dimensional objects or large areas

b *on the way, on the phone* (etc.) and *in the middle* do *not* seem to follow
the same rules.

12

-ence: usually a noun, e.g. experience, prominence, evidence
-ive: usually an adjective, e.g. active, sensitive, creative
-ful: usually an adjective, e.g. wonderful, dreadful, doubtful
-ility: usually a noun, e.g. ability, fertility, availability
-ment: usually a noun, e.g. environment, pavement, excitement
-al: either an adjective, e.g. typical, fundamental, artificial
    or a noun, e.g. survival, recital, trial

13 Money: Teacher's notes

1

a When the students have completed the activity (using dictionaries where necessary), discuss their answers. There is no single correct answer but you should be able to check understanding by their ability to justify their own rankings.

b Same procedure.

c Apart from revising familiar adjectives and consolidating the new vocabulary, this activity will also create the need for certain adjectives which are likely to be new to them, e.g. *generous* and *dishonest*. You could use this situation to teach further adjectives as the need arises.

2

a If the students do not have access to good monolingual dictionaries providing example sentences, you will need to monitor their efforts carefully to avoid mistakes in sentence construction.

3

a When the students have worked out the first part and agreed on an answer, they can look back through the text and focus on new vocabulary, most of which can easily be deduced from the context. You should also highlight certain items on the board which the students may overlook, e.g. to *get money off* (something), *further*, *for ages*, *spend money on* something, etc.

b [cassette] When the students have completed the grid – play the cassette twice if necessary – you could ask them if they have experienced similar problems with any recent purchases.

4

In our experience, multilingual groups spend a vast amount of time comparing the prices of goods in different countries. This activity does no more than provide a structure for such a comparison, but you may find the ensuing discussion taps a rich vein for lexical development, e.g. *double the price, costs twice as much, over-priced, much cheaper* and so on. Before you begin, however, you should check that they understand the vocabulary in the list.

5

a *Hardly ever* is likely to be the only new item here, but you should remind the students of the word order with these adverbs, i.e. before the verb, with the exception of the verb *to be*.

b Tell the students to read through the questions to make sure they understand. You will have to explain *counterfoil* and possibly one or two others as well. The students can then interview a partner or work in small groups. If you detect a significant difference in the answers, you could conclude the activity with a class discussion.

SELF-STUDY ACTIVITIES

1 Although the puzzle hides fourteen currencies, the main vocabulary focus is the different nationalities so make sure your students write these down when they do the activity.
2 You could introduce a problem-solving element in this activity by telling your students to omit the price of each purchase when they compose their text. For example, 'I went into town last weekend and bought a new pen for £X and then . . .'. In the next class students can read out their texts to other members of the class who must guess how much they spent.
3 Students often lack confidence when manipulating numbers and figures in a foreign language. Regular practice of this type can be extremely useful.
4 This is another brief *find out* activity which can generate a lot of discussion and new vocabulary, particularly with a multilingual group.

13 Money: Key words and expressions

Nouns		Verbs	Adjectives
retail price	purse	earn	well-paid
sale	change	win	lucky
fare	salary	inherit	unlucky
tip	inflation rate	give (it) away	generous
carton	exchange rate	invest	careless
copy (of a book)	interest rate	save	dishonest
licence	fare	waste	extravagant
stranger	dozen	borrow	well-off
credit card	oil painting	lend	sensible
counterfoil	pair of shoes	(can't) afford	foolish
cheque	filling	cost	stupid
wallet	petrol	let (a house)	expensive
decanter		rent	medium-priced
coffee maker		carry	
		pay (£5) for it	

Other words and expressions

(ten per cent) off
Value Added Tax (VAT)
a spending spree

reduced from (£9) to (£7)
set of wine glasses
(she) had (£23) left

I almost forgot
   to mention (it)
hardly ever
occasionally

13 **Money:** Key

1

a This is a matter of opinion.

b Again, different people will have different opinions.

c Possibilities are: well-paid, dishonest, lucky, careless, extravagant, generous, well-off, sensible, foolish.

2

a 1 How much did that watch cost?
2 Could I borrow a pen?
3 I'm afraid I can't afford that car.
4 I earn about £15,000 a year.
5 Some friends are going to rent his house.

3

a She ended up with £68.

b

		Problem?	What happened?
1	decanter and glasses	two cracked glasses	got a credit note
2	coffee maker	electrical fault	threw it away
3	scarf	—	lost it
4	computer	couldn't get used to it	sold it to her brother

—— 5 ——

a always
often
quite often
sometimes
occasionally
hardly ever
never

SELF-STUDY ACTIVITIES

1 French franc, Brazilian cruzado, German mark, Indian rupee, Japanese yen, Peruvian sol, Italian lira, Korean won, Greek drachma, South African rand, Dutch guilder, Spanish peseta, Mexican peso, Danish krona.

3 *7½:* seven and a half
VAT: Value Added Tax
£10,000 p.a.: ten thousand pounds per annum
25%: twenty-five per cent
50p: fifty pence

3¾: three and three-quarters
6·75: six point seven five
350: three hundred and fifty
0·8: nought point eight
$4m: four million dollars

14 Entertainment: Teacher's notes

1

a See if the students can work out the answers without any preteaching. Check their answers and clarify meaning where necessary. You will also need to attend to pronunciation, and some classroom drilling would be appropriate for these phrases as they all have a regular stress and intonation pattern, e.g.:

What's it called?
What's it about?

They can then practise the dialogue in pairs.

b When the students have decided upon appropriate questions for a book, film and TV programme, put them into pairs to interview each other on an example of their choice, e.g.:

Have you read *David Copperfield*? (What's it like/about?)
Have you seen *The Last Emperor*? (Where's it on? Who's in it?)

2

a This part should be done individually. Explain any new items, e.g. *dreadful*, at the end.

b Put the students into pairs. Tell them to complete the activity and use their dictionaries to look up any new words from the box. You should, however, give them the correct pronunciation of *livened up*: /laɪvənd ʌp/.

c This could be omitted if you are short of time.

3

a Explain any new vocabulary and practise the pronunciation.

b 🔲 Allow the students several minutes to read through the TV guide before they listen to the tape. Play the passage once and ask the students to compare their answers with a partner's. Monitor the activity carefully and play the tape a second time if they have missed any answers.

c Some of the answers are obvious, others are highly speculative. You could omit this activity if you wish, or you could further exploit the guide in a different way by asking your students to compare it with television in their own country. When doing this, you should point out that this particular guide is for Sunday evening viewing. (*Songs of Praise* and *Highway* are actually religious programmes, and such programmes rarely feature on the other nights in Britain. Would this be true in their own country?)

—— **4** ——

a This exercise highlights two common lexical relationships which are used in the development of spoken and written discourse. The first of these is a part/whole relationship, e.g. *chapter/book* or *painting/exhibition*, and the second is the use of synonymy, e.g. *a bit slow/boring* or *strange/odd*. At the end of the first activity try and elicit these relationships from your students before they practise the dialogue in pairs.

b Do one example with the class to make sure they understand the exercise. When they have finished, check the answers before allowing them to practise the new dialogues.

—— **5** ——

a The first part can be done as a class activity. Students who know the words can explain to other members of the class. You can explain any words that no one else knows. Check understanding by asking the students to write down something they find *dangerous*, *cruel*, etc. This may create the need for vocabulary which appears in **b** and provide you with the ideal opportunity to preteach several new words.

b Put the students into small groups of four or five, and tell them to read through the list and check they understand the meanings of the different phrases (using a dictionary where necessary). They can then discuss the different forms of entertainment, assigning adjectives to each one as they proceed. Allow them, however, to discuss these subjects as freely as they wish.

—— **SELF-STUDY ACTIVITIES** ——

1 This is an opportunity for the students to use the Word building tables at the backs of their books for some simple vocabulary expansion.

14 **Entertainment:** Key words and expressions

Nouns

concert	drama	guitarist	
classical music	serial	soprano	
programme	cartoon	gambling	
orchestra	quiz show	casino	
commercials	soap opera	hunting	
conductor	joke	pin-up magazine	
interval	painting	bullfight	
symphony	musician	stock market	
atmosphere	album	horse races	
channel	chapter	irresponsibility	
(detective) series	exhibition	pornography	
play	audience	weakness	
documentary	team	violence	
comedy	scene		
chat show			

Adjectives

dreadful
loud
religious
great
superb
frightening
marvellous
amazing
off-form

Verbs

liven up
bet

Other words and expressions

Is there (anything) on?	Who's in (it)?	What's (it) like?
What's (it) called?	Who's (it) directed by?	far too long
Who's (it) by?	What's (it) about?	didn't think much of (it)

14 Entertainment: Key

—— 1 ——

a 1 There's a new play starting next week.
2 'The Great White Hope'.
3 Howard Sackler.
4 At the Mermaid Theatre.
5 Hugh Quarshie.
6 Nicolas Kent.
7 Boxing.
8 It sounds very good, but I don't know until I see it.

b 1 'What's on?' for a film or TV programme.
2 'What's it called?' for a book, a film or a TV programme.
3 'Who's it by?' for a book and maybe for a film.
4 'Where's it on?' for a film.
5 'Who's in it?' for a film and a TV programme.
6 'Who's it directed by?' for a film and maybe for a TV programme.
7 'What's it about?' for a book, a film or a TV programme.
8 'What's it like?' for a book, a film or a TV programme.

—— 2 ——

a They are probably talking about a play.

b There are a number of possibilities here but you would probably use these words:
a disco: livened up, stay, loud, went out, music, crowded, atmosphere, noise
a concert: orchestra, singing, stay, conductor, went out, music, interval, symphony
a TV programme: commercials, livened up, changed channels, went out, turned over

—— **3** ——————————————

b ⬛ These are the programmes they talk about; the ones they decide to watch are marked with a star (★):

   International Volleyball – a sports programme
   The News
   Religious programmes
★ The Money Programme – a current affairs programme
★ Galapagos – a wildlife documentary
   Eyes on the Prize – a documentary
   Whicker's World – a documentary about Australia
   Surprise Surprise – a quiz show
★ Wish Me Luck – a drama serial
   Small World – a comedy programme
★ Stanley – a film/documentary
★ Superbowl XXII – a sports programme

—— **4** ——————————————

a

A	*B*
One or two of the <u>actors</u> are a bit <u>weak</u>.	Well, I think most of the <u>cast</u> are pretty <u>poor</u>.
The <u>people</u> in front of me <u>didn't think much</u> of it.	Well, perhaps a lot of the <u>audience</u> <u>felt that way</u>.
There are some good <u>jokes</u> in the first <u>part</u>.	I think the <u>whole</u> thing's very <u>funny</u>, actually.
A couple of the <u>songs</u> are really <u>nice</u>.	I think the whole <u>album's</u> <u>great</u>.
One or two of the <u>paintings</u> are a bit <u>strange</u>.	I think the whole <u>exhibition</u> is very <u>odd</u>.
The first <u>chapter</u> is a bit <u>slow</u>.	I think the whole <u>book's</u> <u>boring</u>, actually.
Some of the <u>musicians</u> are <u>excellent</u>.	Yes, it's a <u>superb</u> <u>orchestra</u>.
Several of the <u>players</u> are a bit <u>off-form</u> at the moment.	The whole <u>team's</u> <u>playing badly</u>, if you ask me.

The underlined words and phrases have a part/whole relationship, e.g. *actors/cast*, or are (near) synonyms, e.g. *weak/poor*.

b These are possible answers:

1 film   terrifying
2 group   odd
3 singers/choir   excellent
4 book   tremendous
5 orchestra   poor

___ **5** ___

b Everyone will have a different opinion here.

___ | SELF-STUDY ACTIVITIES | ___

1 *Adjective*   *Noun*

  a) dangerous   danger
  b) cruel   cruelty
  c) irresponsible   irresponsibility
  d) pornographic   pornography
  e) weak   weakness
  f) violent   violence

2 Some possible adjectives are:
  a book: badly written; well edited.
  a play/film: well acted; badly produced; well directed.

3 1 piano   pianist
  2 cello   cellist
  3 organ/keyboard   organist
  4 trumpet   trumpeter
  5 drum   drummer
  6 guitar   guitarist
  7 saxophone   saxophonist
  8 flute   flautist
  9 violin   violinist

15 **Sport and leisure:** Teacher's notes

1

a When the students have identified the different activities, tell them to move freely around the class for the practice activity. Encourage them to extend the dialogues as they would a normal conversation, i.e. why they enjoy a particular activity, where they do it, etc.

b Some students resort to sentence constructions requiring an adjective and produce the error: 'You need to be *strength*.' You can avoid this error by teaching the adjectives *strong* and *skilful* alongside the respective nouns with the appropriate constructions, e.g.:
You need a lot of strength.
You need to be very strong.

2

a In addition to the use of *have* in these expressions, the students may not be familiar with items such as *swim*, *drink* and *try* used as nouns.

b There are different permutations here, but examples of the *adjective + noun* combinations are *brief look* and *good try*.

3

a Encourage the students to think of different logical ways of completing each sentence, but do not correct any language errors at this stage.

b 🔲 Play the tape and tell the students to write down the answers if they are different from their own completions. You can then discuss both sets of answers (the students' plus the ones on tape) and correct where necessary. Before you begin the free practice, highlight the use of key phrases from the tape, e.g.:

I | play . . . | just for fun
  | do . . . | mostly to keep fit
  | | because I | find it . . .
  | | | enjoy . . . ing . . .
The thing I like about . . . is that it's . . .

4

a Omit this exercise if your students are not interested in football. The students should be able to deduce the meaning of most of the new vocabulary, but you should consolidate their understanding of *although* with further examples.

b There is no single correct answer but the completed lines must be coherent and grammatically correct. Ask the students to compare their texts and comment on the appropriacy of the answers.

5

a Most of these expressions will be familiar but they are a common source of error and the last three phrases are unlikely to be part of the students' active vocabulary. If you feel it is too easy, you could substitute *I doubt it* and *I guess so* for *I don't think so* and *I suppose so*.

b If the subject of sport is not relevant to your students, change the model sentence, e.g. 'Are you going away this weekend?'

6

a Explain any new words and phrases in the box before the students work on the texts. Then put the students into groups to read and discuss the texts. They should use dictionaries to look up new words although you can help them if necessary. At the end the groups can compare and discuss their answers.

b Optional.

SELF-STUDY ACTIVITIES

1 Encourage the students to add to this grid if they are particularly interested in a sport which is not represented here.
2 You could omit this activity if you feel that tennis balls winging their way across the classroom could start a riot. However, it can be great fun.

15 Sport and leisure:
Key words and expressions

Sports and leisure activities

water skiing
climbing
hiking
windsurfing
sailing
riding
skin diving
jogging
bridge
badminton
aerobics
athletics
gardening
hang gliding
chess
squash
yoga
flying
flower arranging

Adjectives

sweaty
televised
stressful
stimulating
relaxing
worried
brief

monotonous
active
creative
voluntary
   (work)
local (club)

Other nouns

strength
skill
stamina
break
penalty
manager
team
champions
result
draw
referee
equaliser
course
vest
foul
goal
match
pharmacist
jazz
musical instrument
workaholic

Other words and expressions

a (2–2) draw
I hope so
I hope not
I think so
I don't think so
I'm afraid so
I'm afraid not
I suppose so
take lessons in (flower
   arranging)
join (a club)
take up (riding)
score
win
compete
have a rest
have a look
have a break
have a try
keep fit
make friends
do something for fun
do something mostly e.g. to
   keep fit; for fun

© Cambridge University Press 1990

15 Sport and leisure: Key

1

a The activities are:

skiing, water skiing, climbing, hiking (walking), windsurfing, camping, sailing, riding, skin diving, jogging.

2

b Here are some possible answers:

1 a *small* party
2 a *good/long* rest
3 a *quick/brief* look
4 a *quick/cold/long/hot* shower
5 a *quick/cold/hot* drink
6 a *quick/brief/long/short* swim
7 a *quick/long/short* break
8 a *good* try

3

a and **b** 🔲 These are some possible endings. The answers from the cassette are underlined:

1 meet people/make friends   4 competing
2 fun   5 relaxing/satisfying/enjoyable
3 keep fit   6 exciting/exhilarating

───── **4** ───────────────────────────────

a Luton FC were held to a 1–1
draw against the Mexican champions
Monterrey, after Hartford scored
the Luton goal just before half-
time. The equaliser came in the sixty-
seventh minute from a penalty.
Although it was a friendly game
there were many fouls and the
referee had to speak to both
captains. Afterwards the Luton
manager said the team played
well enough to win, and he was
disappointed with the final result.

b The missing lines should be something like this:

Cup match, Manchester United lost
In fact, Manchester scored first
the Italians had equalised by half-
the second half and scored
minute. Although Manchester
minutes, they were unable to score.
to play the second leg in Manchester.

───── **5** ───────────────────────────────

a 1 I hope so. I like Mary.
2 I hope not. I don't like Mary.
3 I think so. Somebody told me that she's probably coming.
4 I don't think so. Somebody told me she isn't coming.
5 I'm afraid so. I don't like Mary but I know she's coming.
6 I'm afraid not. I like Mary but she can't come.
7 I suppose so. She usually comes to parties.

b Your answers should be something like this:

1 I hope so. I want to play.
2 I hope not. I don't want to play.
3 I think so. Someone told me I'm probably in the team.
4 I don't think so. Someone told me I'm probably not in the team.
5 I'm afraid so. I'm in the team but I don't want to play.
6 I'm afraid not. I'm not in the team but I'd like to play.
7 I suppose so. I'm usually in the team.

SELF-STUDY ACTIVITIES

1 | *Sport* | *Place* | *Equipment* |
|---|---|---|
| football | pitch | boots, shorts |
| golf | course | clubs |
| tennis | court | racket |
| skiing | slope | sticks, gloves, goggles |
| swimming | pool | trunks, bathing costume, goggles |
| running | track | spikes, shorts, vest |

16 Places: Teacher's notes

—— 1 ——

a It is important that the students understand these words before moving on to the second part of the exercise.

b As this is a much longer activity, you could divide the class into five groups and tell each group to focus on one item, e.g. steel or rice or salt and so on. Each group will need a dictionary and may require your help as well. When they have finished, the groups can compare their answers and students from each group can explain their new vocabulary to other members of the class.

c This can also be done as a class competition. Divide the class into two or three groups and see which group can find the most answers in five minutes.

—— 2 ——

a You could put these phrases on individual slips of paper, give each student one slip of paper, and tell them to move around the class until they find a suitable phrase to complete their sentence. At the end highlight this use of *get* (= become) and add further examples, e.g. *getting warm/cold/ light.* Also check the pronunciation of *mild* /maɪld/ and *pour* /pɔː/.

b Encourage the students to use the new vocabulary in different permutations, e.g.:
It was beginning to get dark.
It was incredibly bright.
It was quite hot.

c This could be set as homework.

—— 3 ——

a Explain the words in the key before you play the tape. When the students have listened once, they can compare their answers. Play the tape a second time if they have not included all the information on their maps.

b Tell the students they can include geographical features not used in **a**. For example, mountains, forests and lakes.

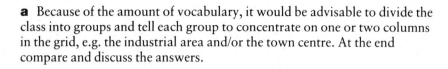

a Because of the amount of vocabulary, it would be advisable to divide the class into groups and tell each group to concentrate on one or two columns in the grid, e.g. the industrial area and/or the town centre. At the end compare and discuss the answers.

b This could be omitted if you are short of time.

a Point out the position of the stress on the penultimate syllable in words ending in *-tion* or *-sion*. There should be no need to explain the words at this stage; some will already be known, others will be clarified by checking in the dictionary, and the gap-filling in **b** should provide adequate contextualisation for matching meanings and dictionary definitions.

b The students can work alone or preferably in pairs. Point out that the verbs in the box will have to be put into the correct tense/form. A few unknown words occur in the dialogue but again the context and other clues should explain the meaning of, for example, *pedestrian precinct, indoor, congested* and so on.

c Clearly this could easily be turned into a longer writing activity in which they could write the whole report. This might be set as homework.

SELF-STUDY ACTIVITIES

1 Students can check their answers to the first part by using the Word building tables on pages 95–105. They will need dictionaries for the second part, as their answers may not be words included in the book.
2 Encourage the students to think in more personalised terms, e.g. places they use and places they don't use; places they like and places they don't like, etc.

16 Places: Key words and expressions

Nouns	Places in a town	Verbs
industry	concert hall	dissolve
agriculture	multi-storey car park	manufacture
mineral	refinery	boil
(chemical) compound	mosque	fry
metal	art gallery	give off (gas)
paddy (field)	coach station	mine
grain	shopping centre	produce
material	bypass	consist of
carbon	temple	cultivate
element	apartment block	put up (an umbrella)
crystal	synagogue	pour (with rain)
(food) processing	opera house	modernize
fuel	ring road	convert
staple diet	sports stadium	renovate
goat		divert
centuries		demolish
iron	**Adjectives**	preserve
climate		widen
thunderstorm	rusty	install
power station	bright	spoil
district	humid	
steel	mild	
coal	incredible	
shade	clear	
sunglasses	showery	
	misty	
	vital	
	congested	

Other words and expressions

in the suburbs   town centre   on the outskirts
throughout the town   in the shade   incredibly e.g. hot
extremely e.g. good

16 Places: Key

<hr>

1

<hr>

a A sheep is an animal.
Steel is a metal.
Coal is a mineral.
Rice is a plant.
Salt is a chemical compound.

b *A sheep:* 2, 14, 16, 18, 23
It is sometimes kept on farms.
It is important for its meat and its wool.
It can live on very poor grass.
Its milk can be used for cheese production.
It is related to the goat.

Steel: 3, 8, 11, 15, 25
It is used in many manufacturing industries.
It gets rusty.
It is a very strong material.
It does not burn.
It is produced from iron.

Coal: 5, 10, 13, 20, 21
It is brown or black.
When it burns, it gives off smoke.
It contains carbon and other elements.
It is used as a fuel.
It is mined.

Rice: 4, 7, 9, 22, 24
It is boiled or fried before being eaten.
It is grown in paddies.
It is a grain.
It is the staple diet in many countries.
It has been cultivated for centuries.

Salt: 1, 6, 12, 17, 19
It dissolves in water.
Its chemical formula is NaCl.
It is sometimes mined and sometimes produced from sea water.
It consists of crystals.
It is used in food processing.

c Some examples are:

1 wheat, barley
2 silver, gold
3 oil
4 cat, spider
5 any weeds or wild flowers
6 concrete, brick
7 quartz
8 lion, frog
9 bleach
10 sand, petrol

——— 2 ———————————————————

a One possible set of answers is:

It was getting hot so I decided to sit in the shade.
It was very bright so I put on my sunglasses.
It was getting dark so I put the lights on.
It was beginning to rain so I put my umbrella up.
It was incredibly humid so I decided to take a shower.
It was pouring with rain so I couldn't go out.
It was quite mild so I didn't take my overcoat.
It was extremely icy so I decided not to go by car.

c There may be lots of places like this, but we had Korea in mind.

——— 3 ———————————————————

a The map should look something like this:

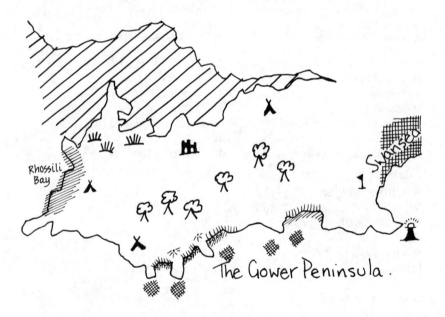

—— 4

a The answers will be different for different towns and countries.

—— 5

a diversion; installation; renovation; conversion; extension; modernisation; demolition; preservation.

b These are possible answers:

1	improved, modernised	8 demolished
2	turned	9 installed
3	converted	10 renovated
4	replaced	11 spoilt
5	extend	12 improved
6	diverted	13 preserved
7	widen	

SELF-STUDY ACTIVITIES

1 rusty, icy, sunny, showery, misty, ugly.

3 The answers (with the bigger first):
lake – pond; mountain – hill; forest – wood; farm – field; river – stream; factory – workshop; lane – path; barn – shed.

17 **Bureaucracy:** Teacher's notes

1

The unit contains a number of compounds relevant to this exercise, so you could do it at the end and use it for revision.

2

a When the students prepare their question forms, tell them they are not forbidden to use vocabulary already contained in the form; in some cases it may be quite natural, e.g. 'What's your date of birth?' This is a perfectly natural question in spoken English. In most cases, however, the question in spoken English is likely to deviate from the more formal vocabulary, e.g. 'How long are you staying?' (not 'What's the length of your visit?'). Put the different possibilities on the board and discuss the differences before playing the tape.

b 🔲 This could be combined with **c**. Ask one student to listen for the information and fill in the form, while a partner writes down the question forms. The pairs could then role-play the interview.

d This activity may be unnecessary if you have adopted the above approach.

3

a This exercise is an excellent way to follow up a lesson on modal verbs of obligation as it allows free practice of *have to*, *should* and *don't have to*.
   Ask the students to read through the information and clarify any problems with meaning. A number of items may be new, although the meaning is often self-explanatory, e.g. *take out* and *register*. You will need to check pronunciation, e.g. *certificate* /sətɪfɪkət/ and *advertisement* /ədvɜːtɪsmənt/.

b Put the students into pairs or small groups for the speaking activity. Although this activity may not hold the same fascination for a monolingual group, it is not uncommon to find disagreements between students from the same country about what one should or should not do.

4

a Follow the instructions in the Student's Book and clarify meaning where necessary.

b This is ideal for pair work and, in the process of matching words with pictures, the students will be rehearsing the whole narrative (in preparation for **c**).

c In the same pairs, tell the students to invent two more pieces of information for the narrative, e.g. 'When I was filling in my enrolment form in reception, I met an old friend.' You can then change the pairs and ask each student to read the story (with additional information) to their new partner.

d An optional activity. We have found that it can generate a lot of discussion with certain groups.

5

a You could write additional examples on the board to illustrate the meaning of *unless*. Check the students' sentences carefully before moving on.

b Don't preteach new vocabulary; allow the pairs to discover the meaning for themselves (using a dictionary and the context) as they discuss the sentences. When they have finished, you could discuss the answers with the whole group.

c When the pairs have finished, you could ask them to move round the class and choose the best paraphrase for each notice.

SELF-STUDY ACTIVITIES

1 This writing exercise offers an opportunity for consolidation of vocabulary learned in the previous exercise. It will also require attention to the use of sequencing words and phrases to avoid boring repetition of *And then . . .*, etc.
2 This activity may be of practical use to the students and could be developed into a whole collection of common notices and their equivalents in the mother tongue.
3 A bilingual dictionary will allow the students to investigate areas of personal interest.

17   Bureaucracy: Key words and expressions

Nouns

(application) form	embassy	election	
(birth) certificate	document	crash helmet	
surname	dose	military	
occupation	examination	service	
injection	advertisement	employer	
visa	vaccination	permission	
insurance	fee	prison	
work permit	receipt	resident	
	queue	premises	
	enrolment form	patron	
	accounts		

Verbs

sign
register
open (an
    account)
enrol
hang around
queue
fill in (forms)
(not) be allowed
    to
vote
exceed

Other words and expressions

country of origin
Where are you from?
marital status
permanent address
temporary address
length of visit
purpose of visit
date of birth
What's your name?
Are you married?
What do you do?

Where do you live?
How long are you staying?
Why are you here?
When were you born?
international driving licence
a waste of time
in the wrong place
first of all
out of order
eventually

Adjectives

temporary
permanent
medical
valid
furious
unauthorised

© Cambridge University Press 1990

17 Bureaucracy: Key

1

Some of the common compounds are:

credit card	driving licence	application	birth certificate
birthday card	TV licence	form	death certificate
boarding card	gun licence	booking	doctor's certificate
membership card	import licence	form	vaccination
cheque card		enrolment	certificate
		form	exam certificate

2

a Some possible spoken questions are:

What's your surname/family name?
What's your first name?
When were you born?
Where do you come from? / Where are you from?
What do you do (for a living) / What's your job/occupation?
Are you married (single or divorced)?
Where do you live?
Where are you living/staying at the moment/at present?
Why are you here? / Why have you come here? / What are you here for?
How long are you staying? / How long do you intend to stay?

b

Surname: Bajan
Forename: Sonia
Date of birth: 3 February 1961
Country of origin: Switzerland
Occupation: Bank employee
Marital status: Married

Permanent address: Richttanne, 8627 Gruningen
Temporary address: 18 Brackley Road, London W4
Purpose of visit: General language course
Length of stay: Five and a half months
Date: 13th ....

c 📼 The interviewer's questions in the same order as on the recording:

Let's start with your name. . . . That's your first name?
And your family name?
Where are you from?
So you're married then?
What do you do in Switzerland?
Whereabouts do you live in Switzerland? . . . What's the address?
Where are you staying here in England? . . . What's the address?
What are you here for exactly?
How long will you be here for?
How old are you? . . . When were you born?

—— **5** —————————————————————

c Here are possible answers:

1 You can only eat food here which you have bought here.
2 The lift is not working at the moment.
3 Only for people staying at the hotel.
4 No entry for people without official permission.
5 Do not take more (of this medicine) than it says on the label.

18 Revision and expansion:
Teacher's notes

—— 1 ——

You could ask the students to write their answers on a piece of paper. When they have finished, each student puts their paper on the floor in the centre of the room. Shuffle the papers and then tell each student to take one. The aim is for them to try and guess whose paper they have.

—— 2 ——

This could also be done in small groups or as a class quiz with two teams.

—— 3 ——

This is a similar exercise to exercise 7 in Unit 6; see the comment on page 36.

—— 4 ——

You could also ask the students to pick out the errors which could result from interference from their own mother tongue.

—— 5 ——

We have tried to include common uses of *get* throughout the book in the hope that students will begin to get a *feel* for the use of this important English verb. Exercise **a** draws together the important uses of *get* and **b** provides further consolidation. If students have difficulty with **b**, give them an example.

—— 6 ——

a This exercise alerts students to two common features of English:

1 The use of numbers to form compound adjectives.
2 Zero affixation, i.e. common words which can be used in different word classes without any change in form.

b In this exercise the transformation from verb to noun will demand the inclusion of a second verb. Knowledge of the correct verb is being tested here.

—— **7** ——

This exercise provides further explanation of the Word building tables at the back of the book – as do exercises 9 and 10.

—— **8** ——

This could be a writing activity given as homework.

18 Revision and expansion:
New words and expressions

Nouns	Other words and expressions	
health	give (her) a ring	I'm not really interested in (it)
ring	give (her) an interview	under stress
	give (her) a fine	essential
	have fun	
	I'm not very keen on (it)	
	I quite like (running)	

—— **2** ————————————————————

Here are their nationalities and professions/occupations:

Meryl Streep: American film actress
Germaine Greer: Australian writer
Diego Maradonna: Argentinian footballer
Melina Mercouri: Greek politician
Gabriel García Márquez: Colombian author/novelist
Florence Griffith Joyner: American athlete
Said Aouita: Moroccan athlete
Toshiro Mifune: Japanese actor
Severiano Ballesteros: Spanish golfer
Steffi Graf: West German tennis player
Andrei Sakharov: Soviet physicist/dissident
Benazir Bhutto: Prime Minister of Pakistan
Ingmar Stenmark: Swedish skier
Corazon Aquino: President of the Philippines
Yo-Yo Ma: Chinese cellist
Winnie Mandela: South African political activist
Edith Piaf: French singer
Giorgio Armani: Italian fashion designer
Gérard Depardieu: French film actor
Jessye Norman: American opera singer
Milton Nascimento: Brazilian singer
Kyung-Wha Chung: Korean violinist
Satyajit Ray: Indian film producer and director
Mother Teresa: Indian Roman Catholic nun, working in Calcutta
    (born in Yugoslavia of Albanian parents)

4
---

1 He is very stressed.
2 Could you lend me £50? / Could I borrow £50?
3 I hardly ever go to the cinema. / I almost never go to the cinema.
4 Do you do any sport?
5 I enjoy swimming.
6 We produce a lot of steel in my country.
7 Bring your homework tomorrow and give it to me at lunchtime.
8 I'm not very keen on classical music.
9 What is it like?
10 There's an exhibition at the National Gallery next week.
11 The film was awful – I was really bored. / It was really boring.
12 I like tennis; it's fun.

5
---

a The synonyms are:

1 get to = arrive at   4 get = buy
2 get = obtain   5 get = become
3 get = fetch

b Here are some possible answers:

1 Don't worry. I'll go and get them for you. (fetch)
2 No, if you're sure it will get there by Friday. (arrive)
3 Yes, if we get a taxi. (take)
4 No, but I'll get a loan from the bank. (obtain)
5 Thanks. I got it from that new shop in the High Street. (bought)

6
---

a Some examples are:

a ten-hour drive; a five-minute rest; a twenty-minute interview;
a two-day wait; a fifteen-mile walk; a thousand-pound fine.

≫→

b Some examples are:

He *bandaged* her leg.   He *put a bandage* on her leg.
He *looked* at the problem.   He *had a look* at the problem.
She *tipped* the waiter.   She *gave* the waiter *a tip*.
She *sacked* them all.   She *gave* them all *the sack*.
She *checked* them thoroughly.   She *gave* them *a* thorough *check*.

—— **7** ——————————————————————

a -able   adjectives, as in 'predictable'
   -ness   nouns, as in 'happiness'
   -y   adjectives, as in 'windy'
   -ment   nouns, as in 'improvement'
   -ous   adjectives, as in 'disastrous'
   -sion   nouns, as in 'expression'

© Cambridge University Press 1990

Tapescripts

Unit 1 Learning

Exercise 6

Check your pronunciation.

comfortable	rug	on purpose
recipe	equals	cover
guess	tongue	improve

oven	sewing
lettuce	nightmare
phrase	

Unit 2 Around the house

Exercise 4b

Listen to the conversation and fill in the table in your book.

M: A lot of English people don't like living in flats, but I think . . . er . . . one of the nice things about being high up – and I live on the eighth floor – is that you get a nice view. (mm) Where I am it's great: lovely view overlooking the city and er . . . the river in the background . . . and it's really quiet because you hardly hear the noise of the traffic and everything when you're eight floors up.

W: There must be some things you don't like though?

M: Yeah. I miss not having a garden. When I was a little kid we had . . . er . . . oh, huge garden with a pond and rockery and everything; it was great. But all I've got now is a tiny little balcony where I can only grow a few flowers.

I think probably it's also harder to get to know people in a block of flats. I don't know but . . . somehow it's more impersonal than being in a nice little street with houses on either side. And then there's the great fear that I have, that one day the, the lift will break down with me inside. I'm really quite frightened of going in lifts but . . . well, on the eighth floor you've really no choice. I thought I'd get used to it but I haven't.

W: Well, I prefer living in a house – especially a detached house, because you've got so much more privacy. And then there's the garden. When I sit in the lounge or the kitchen I can look out onto the garden and almost imagine I'm in the country. I . . . I'd hate to be stuck in a flat at the top of a skyscraper with nothing but concrete all around me.

I guess the only thing that worries me about it is that it's a bit of a security risk. I mean . . . burglars could easily get round the back of the house if they wanted to, so there are lots of doors and windows that I really have to protect very carefully . . . you know, lots of locks and things. We've got a big dog, but I still worry about it.

M: But that's the only thing you don't like about the house?

W: Mm . . . yes, I think so . . . well, at least, that's all that comes to mind.

Unit 2, Exercise 7

Check your pronunciation.

chest of drawers	wardrobe
cupboard	corkscrew
washbasin	I'll switch it off

flour	saucepan
towel	stale
lounge	he does the ironing

Unit 3 Clothes and shopping

Exercise 5b

Listen to Bob talking about his visit to the department store and answer the questions in your book.

Bob: Well, I went with my wife, Jean, and first of all we went straight to the furniture department on the top floor and ordered a bed. Then we went down a floor so Jean could go to the record department and get a cassette she wanted. So I left her there while I bought a . . . a novel and a couple of other books – I thought one of them would make a nice present for Ted – and as the stationery department was just next door I got a note pad and some envelopes at the same time.

Anyway, I went back and found Jean buying more toys for our two nephews so I quickly dragged her away and headed for the lift to take us to the sportswear department; I wanted to buy a tracksuit for jogging and have a look at some exercise bicycles as well. Jean wasn't very interested so she went on down to the ladieswear department to look at some clothes. We met up again in the bedding department because we had to get some sheets, and then . . . er . . . went back down to the ground floor where I got some toothpaste in toiletries and . . . er . . . Jean went and bought some needles and thread.

Anyway, we finished up in the basement; we bought a kettle and some knives and forks and . . . er . . . oh, one or two things and as we were there we decided to have a cup of coffee. That was when I suddenly remembered I forgot to buy underwear when I was up in the menswear department.

Unit 3, Exercise 7

Check your pronunciation.

gloves	necklace	leather
tie	bracelet	suit
brooch	blouse	suede

among
tidy
I'm being served, thanks

Unit 4 Food and drink

Exercise 3b

Listen and answer the questions in your book.

W: . . . and then of course we went out last night.
M: Oh yes, what was it like?
W: Very nice . . . I'd definitely recommend it. But if you want to go, you'll probably need to book, because it gets very busy, especially at the weekend. We didn't bother as it was a Tuesday, but even so, there were quite a few people there.
M: And the food was good?
W: Yeah, excellent. We had a slight problem to start with because they put us at a table near a window which was a bit draughty, but when we asked for another table they were very nice about it, and after that the service was great. Anyway, we had an aubergine dish to start, with a yoghurt sauce and masses of garlic. And then for the main course I had lamb, which was very tender, and the others had some kind of casserole – pieces of pork marinated in oil and herbs and lemon juice (mmm!) and then cooked with onions and peppers and so on. And we finished with one of those sticky-sweet desserts made from nuts and honey.
M: Mmm. Sounds nice. Is it pricey?
W: Well, it's about fifteen pounds each I guess, which isn't bad when you

consider that we had a bottle of wine, coffee and Greek brandy at the end of the meal, and the other two had aperitifs as well *and* service is included so you don't need to give a tip.

M: Yeah, that's not bad these days. I think I'll give it a try. Where did you say it was exactly?

Unit 4, Exercise 6

Check your pronunciation.

cabbage	cauliflower
pineapple	onions
pear	strawberry
peas	

look at the menu	half a million
average	rare
nine point two one	hangover

Unit 5 People and relationships

Exercise 3c

Listen to Paul talking about his marriage and put 'true' or 'false' beside the sentences in your book.

P: Well, I guess things started to go wrong just after we had Tom – er that's the baby. We both knew it was going to be difficult but well it was the flat really; it just wasn't big enough for the three of us, so when the baby cried – seemed to be crying all the time, of course – it disturbed us both during the day and kept both of us awake at night and somehow we simply couldn't get away from it and have any time to ourselves. Anyway, after a while I started to lose my temper very quickly – you know, easily – not with the baby I . . . I don't mean; no, I was very calm and patient when I was actually looking after him; but I used to lose my temper

with Jane and we had terrible arguments and . . .

W: Physical?

P: No, no, no, no, nothing like that; I never touched Jane but . . . I used to shout at her and smash things and . . . at first she shouted back at me, but after a while she responded by spending more and more time with the baby and she just ignored me. And when I saw her giving all her attention to the baby, I . . . I suppose I was jealous of him and I felt very lonely.

W: And did you tell Jane about your feelings?

P: I tried – well, once or twice I tried, but there never seemed to be time and when there was, we were both too tired. Anyway, er . . . eventually I . . . I left; I . . . I just couldn't stand it; and we finally got divorced last year.

W: How do you feel about it now?

P: I regret it; I regret it very much. But, looking back on it, I think we were probably too young. I mean, I don't think I was ready for the baby and things.

Unit 5, Exercise 7

Check your pronunciation.

illegal	stare
illegible	miserable
impatient	nervous
embarrassed	fall in love

library	jealous
familiar	ignore
married	favour
divorced	promise

Unit 7 Time

Exercise 1b

Listen carefully to the correct sentences.

1 How long are you staying?
2 I saw him last night. *or* I saw him yesterday evening.

3 I didn't sleep very well last night.
4 I haven't seen her for three weeks.
5 What are you doing tonight?
6 When did you arrive in London?
7 I arrived two days ago.
8 What time shall we meet?
9 I'm going there next month.
10 Before leaving we must get some souvenirs.
11 I haven't seen her in the last few days.
12 I'm going to the shop but I'll be back in half an hour.

Unit 7, Exercise 6

Check your pronunciation.

occasionally	adolescent
punctual	youth
for a while	adult

go bald	Is that convenient?
lose weight	nineteen seventy-five
Is it urgent?	ten minutes ago

Unit 8 Holidays and travel

Exercise 3b

Listen to these examples.

1 A: It was freezing, wasn't it?
  B: Yeah, it was very cold.

2 A: Delicious food, wasn't it?
  B: Yeah, it was very good.

Now you go on. Reply to each question in a similar way.

3 A: It was enormous, wasn't it?
4 A: It was filthy, wasn't it?
5 A: Oh, the flat was tiny, wasn't it?
6 A: And it was ancient, wasn't it?
7 A: Oh, it was an awful journey, wasn't it?
8 A: And we were exhausted, weren't we?

Unit 8, Exercise 6

Check your pronunciation.

departure lounge	travel agency
holiday resort	luggage
excess baggage	enquiry

foreign	harbour
abroad	yacht
mountains	sunbathe

Unit 9 Transport

Exercise 1a

Look at the map and find the place which says 'You start here'. Now follow the directions.

M: Go along this road, turn . . . er . . . left at the traffic lights, erm, and then take the . . . the, oh, the, the second on the right. You'll see the bus stop on the, on the left hand side, just after the cinema.

Mark the bus stop on your map and follow the next set of directions. Remember you are now at the bus stop.

W: OK. Now you keep going along this road in the same direction. Then you turn right at the main road and then take the second on the left. Yes, that's right and you'll see the bank about halfway along on the opposite side of the road.

Mark the bank on your map and follow the next set of directions.

M: Go back down this road . . . er . . . turn left and then keep going for, er, oh, er, um, about five minutes. The underground's on your left . . . er . . . er, it's just before you get to the roundabout.

Mark the underground on your map and follow the final set of directions.

W: OK. Take the road on your right at the roundabout, and then turn right again when you get to a T-junction.

Now, when you've done that, you've got to follow the road, past a church, over a set of traffic lights, and then take the next road on your left. The restaurant's about, oh, halfway along on the right-hand side.

Mark the restaurant on your map.

Unit 9, Exercise 6

Check your pronunciation.

buffet car	baggage
ticket office	package
lost property office	slightly damaged

badly injured	ambulance
pedestrian crossing	rowing boat
parked cars	

Unit 10 Work

Exercise 3b

Listen to the interview and fill in the table in your book.

M: Well, now then, one thing I'd like to ask is . . . er . . . exactly why you applied for the job; I mean, just looking at your application form, you're actually overqualified . . .

W: Yes, I thought you might ask that. Erm . . . the thing is, in my present job, although I'm actually in charge of a small team and I have a lot of responsibility, it's largely a desk job with a lot of paperwork . . .

M: You're not too keen on being stuck in an office all day?

W: To be honest, no. I much prefer being out on site where I can supervise things, and deal with problems as they occur. And this job should give me that kind of contact with other engineers, architects, builders and so on.

M: Mmm. You'd certainly have to do quite a lot of travelling in the local area, you know, visiting different

sites. You do realise, though, that the starting salary isn't as good as the salary in your present job?

W: Yes, I realise that, but erm . . . it does say in the job advertisement that the promotion prospects are very good.

M: That's true, and er . . . as this is a new project we're working on, we think there'll be a very good chance of fairly quick promotion, depending on performance, that is . . .

W: Yes, of course. Well, you see, I've got very little chance of promotion in my present job. I mean it's a very small company and there's really nowhere for me to go; that's why I'm looking around for somewhere else.

Unit 10, Exercise 6

Check your pronunciation.

mechanic	photographer
secretary	journalist
lawyer	architect

creative	diary	efficient
skilled	client	sociable
unpleasant	organised	reliable

Unit 11 Crime

Exercise 3b

Listen and answer the questions in your book.

M: Well, I was just standing in a queue waiting to be served, when I heard er . . . I . . . heard this shout behind me. So I turned round and there were two guys standing at the door; one of them had a gun and, erm . . . you know . . . he was er . . . he was pointing this shotgun at us.

W: Only one had a gun?

M: Er . . . yes, yes, I think so, though I really couldn't be sure; you know

what it's like. And they were both
wearing some kind of stocking over
their heads so I couldn't really see
what they looked like, but er . . .
they were both about medium
height, probably in their twenties,
I'd say, judging by their clothes, but
again I couldn't be sure. Anyway,
they told us all to lie down on the
floor, and a guy at the front of the
queue told the cashier to start
putting the money into a bag he was
carrying.

W: And he was at the front of the
queue?

M: Yeah, er, yeah, he was one of the
gang, but em . . . well, he was already
in the bank when the others came in.

W: And did you get a good look at him?

M: No. I never saw his face because he
was in front of me in the queue, you
see. And, anyway, the next thing . . .
the alarm went off. I guess it must
have been one of the other cashiers
that set it off; then there was panic.
Several people started to get up,
somebody screamed, and then the
gun went off – it was terrifying, and
I could just see out of the corner of
my eye someone crashing to the
floor. I . . . I guess the robbers must
have panicked, too, at this point,
because, er . . . well, they just rushed
out, and . . . well, that was it. The
only thing I recall after that was
that when I got up, the cashier was
still just standing there holding this
brown bag in his hands – terrified.

Unit 11, Exercise 6

Check your pronunciation.

thief	the bomb went off
burglary	seriously injured
average	cause
damage	conveyor belt
guilty	official
suitcase	terminal

Unit 13 Money

Exercise 3b

Listen and fill in the table in your book.

M: . . . this afternoon, I thought I'd get
a few things in the sale.

W: Well, be careful. I bought loads of
things in the January sales and some
of them, well, turned out to be a bit
of a disaster.

M: Yeah?

W: Yeah. I got a decanter and a set of
wine glasses, and when I got home
and unpacked them, I discovered
that two of them had a little crack in
them.

M: Did you take them back?

W: Yeah, but you can't get your money
back on sale goods; all I got was a
credit note, which wasn't much use
'cause there was nothing else I
wanted to buy.

M: Yeah, that's always the case.

W: And do you remember that coffee
maker I told you about?

M: Er . . . I think so, yeah.

W: Well, *that* never worked properly;
something wrong with the electrics;
in the end I threw it away.

M: Oh, what a shame.

W: Well, I suppose that's the risk you
take. I got a lovely jacket and skirt
and I wear *them* all the time.
Unfortunately, I lost the scarf I got
to go with them, but um . . . oh . . .
and the oil painting I got is really
one of my favourite things.

M: The one beside the bookcase in the
living room?

W: Yeah. I got that in a sale. I love it –
wish I could say the same about that
computer; couldn't get the hang of
it at all. I sold it to my brother in the
end.

M: Really. I've been thinking of getting
a computer for ages.

W: Well, that's probably a good thing
to buy in the sales.

Unit 13, Exercise 6

Check your pronunciation.

I can't afford it	wallet
inherit	reduce
purse	I got ten per cent off

quite often
a packet of cigarettes
television licence
half a dozen

Unit 14 Entertainment

Exercise 3b

Listen to the conversation and answer the questions in your book.

W: What's on the box tonight?

M: Er . . . let's see . . . well, there's volleyball at the moment. Er . . . we've missed almost half of that. There's the news in a couple of minutes, followed by the usual religious programmes on a Sunday or . . . *The Money Programme*?

W: Oh, that's quite interesting. What's it about tonight?

M: Er . . . it's something to do with the problems they're having with a new petrol. Apparently they've just taken it off the market.

W: Mmm. Well, that sounds OK. Let's watch that. And after?

M: Well, I'd quite like to see the wildlife documentary at seven fifteen. There isn't much else on at that time actually, unless you er . . . unless you want to watch *Eyes on the Prize*.

W: Oh, that thing about Kennedy and civil rights during the sixties. No thank you.

M: OK, fine. Well, at eight fifteen there's a documentary about British people in Australia. Er . . . a quiz show – you know, that thing on the Stock Market? Or that drama serial we saw last week.

W: Oh, the one about the Second World War?

M: Mmm.

W: Erm, what's it called?

M: *Wish Me Luck*.

W: That's it. Yes. That was quite good. Let's watch that.

M: Yes. There's nothing much on after that that you'll like. Um, *Small World* – you know, the comedy programme we saw last week, remember?

W: Yes. Isn't there a chat show at ten o'clock?

M: Mmm. No. Oh, hang on though; it says here there's a film about the artist Stanley Spencer which is very good. 'A moving story and also very funny' according to this guide.

W: At ten?

M: Mmm.

W: Oh well, fine. That'll take me up to bed time. And at least there are no soap operas on, on a Sunday.

M: Yeah. I might stay up and watch the Superbowl, actually.

W: What – are they showing the highlights?

M: No. It' the whole thing live from America.

W: Oh, well, in that case I definitely will have an early night.

Unit 14, Exercise 6

dreadful	orchestra	cruel
liven up	symphony	musician
conductor	violent	exhibition

audience	guitarist
superb	
pianist	

Unit 15 Sport and leisure

Exercise 3b

Listen and complete the sentences in your book.

1
M: Well, I haven't really got any hobbies, but er . . . I've only recently moved to this area, so I decided to join this Bridge Club, because I thought it might be a good way to meet people . . . . To tell you the truth, I haven't really made many friends, but I do enjoy bridge . . . very much . . . so it's been quite good for me.

2
W: I play quite a lot of badminton actually . . . just for fun; I don't believe in taking sport too seriously. You know, some people get very aggressive when they play team games. I hate that.

3
W: I suppose my main relaxation is aerobics – if you can call it relaxation. I do it twice a week, mostly to keep fit, because I'm in a desk job and I really don't get that much exercise unless I force myself to do something energetic.

4
M: Well, I play a lot of football in the winter, mostly for pleasure – nothing serious. But my main sport is athletics and I think the thing I like about it is er . . . well, I . . . I enjoy competing against other people, and er . . . oh, I get a lot of satisfaction when I win!

5
M: I spend most of my free time in the garden. There always seems to be something that needs doing, but I don't mind; I enjoy it. I find it very relaxing and very satisfying.

6
W: My latest craze is hang gliding, and the thing I love about it is that it's so exciting. You just can't imagine, unless you actually do it, what it's like to just float in space hundreds of feet up. It's fabulous.

Unit 15, Exercise 7

Check your pronunciation.

strength	sweaty	foul
hiking	a draw	penalty
climbing	equaliser	I suppose so

photography	unemployed
advertising	musical instrument
monotonous	voluntary

Unit 16 Places

Exercise 3a

Listen to the conversation and follow the instructions in your book.

G: Well, I'd like to help a bit more but it's a long time since I've been there; not since I was a kid, you know. I'm not sure how much I remember.
L: Well, for instance, what are the beaches like? I mean are they sandy or stony?
G: Mm, a bit of both, as far as I remember, but the one at the left in the west is a long sandy one – called Rhossili if I remember.
L: Ah, yes, the long bay with headlands at the ends. And that's nice, is it, that beach?
G: Oh, yes. It's got dunes behind it and we used to . . . you know, kids love playing and hiding in sand dunes, don't they? You get a nice wind from the sea – off the Atlantic, I suppose. A nice fresh breeze.
L: What about the rest of the coastline? Is it good for walking?
G: Well, now . . . in the south there are a few nice little bays – sandy and

some with pebbles, I think. Oh, yes, and it's quite steep down to the sea. Actually, there are cliffs along there, I think, with a footpath at the top and quite a lot of rocks down below in the sea; and I think you can see some islands further away in the sea. Anyway, it's a nice view with the waves breaking over the rocks and the sea and everything. And then north of Rhossili, behind where the dunes are, there's a very flat marshy area. That's right; it's actually a river mouth up there.

L: Is there any way across to the mainland there? I mean a ferry or anything?

G: No, no. It's all mud flats, I'm afraid. It might be good for bird watching or shellfish or something but that's all. You can't walk over it or anything.

L: What's it like at the Swansea end of the peninsula?

G: Mmm. Swansea's a big city. The beach is long but, er, not that nice and the whole area is built up. The whole of that end is built up actually, so I suppose it's OK, but not really the place for a holiday.

L: Mmm.

G: Inland there are one or two ancient ruins – like castles – but I can't remember whether they're worth seeing. There's one just south of the marshes, I remember. The villages aren't particularly pretty but, er, there are some woodlands.

L: What, you mean like forests?

G: Well, woods rather than forests; nothing much really. It's a bit hilly and quite wild really. I seem to remember there's some kind of golf course near Swansea though. Derek will be interested in that no doubt.

L: Yes, but it's mainly the coast that's worth seeing, is it?

G: Mm, I suppose so. There's even a lighthouse on the headland south of Swansea. If you're going in the camper, there's plenty of places to stay – several camp sites.

L: Well, that's really useful. Thanks very much for your help. We'll let you see the photos when we get back.

Unit 16, Exercise 6

Check your pronunciation.

island
wind
mild
The Atlantic Ocean
castle

village
humid
footpath
industry
a chemical compound

material	iron
substance	pouring with rain
food processing	statue
fuel	museum
staple diet	library
	mosque
	synagogue

Unit 17 Bureaucracy

Exercise 2b

Listen and answer the questions in your book.

M: Right. If I could just ask you a few questions; erm . . . let's start with your name.

W: It's Sonia.

M: Sonia. That's your first name?

W: Yes.

M: OK. And your family name?

W: It's Bajan.

M: Bajan. How do you spell that?

W: B-A-J-A-N.

M: Right. OK. And where are you from, Sonia?

W: From Switzerland.

M: From Switzerland.
W: Yes.
M: Bajan's not a very Swiss name, is it?
W: No, it isn't. It's Hungarian.
M: Hungarian?
W: Yes.
M: Is your family Hungarian?
W: No. It's my husband's family.
M: Oh, I see. Right, so you're married then?
W: Yes.
M: OK. And what do you do in Switzerland?
W: I work in a bank.
M: In a bank. Right. And whereabouts do you live in Switzerland?
W: Near Zurich.
M: Near Zurich. OK. Er . . . what's the address?
W: It's Richttanne.
M: Er . . . could you spell that please?
W: Yes. R-I-C-H-double T-A-double N-E.
M: OK. I've got that.
W: And it's 8627 Gruningen.
M: Gruningen. I've heard that before; I know that. OK. Right, and where are you staying here in England?
W: In London.
M: In London. With a family?
W: Yes.
M: OK. What's the address?
W: It's 18 Brackley Road.
M: Brackley?
W: Brackley Road.
M: Yeah.
W: W4. London W4.
M: Fine. OK. And what are you here for exactly?
W: Oh, I'm doing a general language course.
M: In a . . . in a language school?
W: Yes.
M: I see. Erm . . . your English sounds pretty good to me. Er . . . how long er . . . how long will you be here for?
W: Five and a half months.
M: Five and a half months?
W: Yes.

M: That's quite a long time. It's nice. Er . . . right, I think that's about all . . . erm . . . oh yes, sorry; one thing: how old are you, Sonia?
W: I'm twenty-six.
M: OK. And when were you born?
W: It's the third of February, 1961.
M: Three two sixty-one.
W: Sixty-one.
M: OK. I think that's about all. Erm . . . could you just put your signature here for me, please?
W: Yes, of course.
M: Fine. And the date.
W: It's the thirteenth?
M: Thir . . . thirteenth, yes. That's it. Lovely. Thanks very much.

Unit 17, Exercise 6

Check your pronunciation.

traveller's cheques
medical insurance
international driving licence
embassy
advertisement

birth certificate
vaccination certificate
furious
receipt
eventually

queue
vote
military service
you're not allowed to